Contents

Chairmen's Introductions		2
Acknowledgements		5
Rights of Way Information		7
Key to Map Symbols		7
Public Transport Information		8
The Country Code		60
Maps and Directions:		
Section 1:	part 1a - Pangbourne to Little Heath - 7km	10
	1b - Little Heath to Burghfield Bridge - 6km	12
Section 2:	part 2a - Burghfield Bridge to Grazely - 6km	14
	2b - Grazely to The Devil's Highway - 6km	16
	2c - The Devil's Highway to Padworth - 7km	18
Section 3:	part 3a - Padworth to Tadley - 6km	20
	3b - Tadley to Goose Hill - 6km	22
	3c - Goose Hill to Greenham Common - 5.5km	24
Section 4:	part 4a - Greenham Common to Wash Water - 7km	26
	4b - Wash Water to Heath End - 6km	28
	4c - Heath End to Walbury Hill - 5.5km	30
Section 5:	part 5a - Walbury Hill to Lower Slope End Farm - 7km	32
	5b - Lower Slope End Farm to Hungerford - 6km	34
Section 6:	part 6a - Hungerford to Straight Soley - 7km	36
	6b - Straight Soley to Lambourn Woodlands - 6.5km	38
Section 7:	part 7a - Lambourn Woodlands to Lambourn Corner - 6km	40
	7b - Lambourn Corner to Seven Barrows - 6.5km	42
Section 8:	part 8a - Seven Barrows to Grange Farm - 5km	44
	8b - Grange Farm to Fawley Monument - 5km	46
Section 9:	part 9a - Fawley Monument to Lands End - 7km	48
	9b - Lands End to Gore Hill - 5km	50
	9c - Gore Hill to Compton - 6km	52
Section 10:	part 10a - Compton to Warren Farm - 5km	54
	10b - Warren Farm to Lower Basildon - 8km	56
	10c - Lower Basildon to Pangbourne - 4.5km	58

The Chairman's Walk

The idea

There is a tradition that each chairman of West Berkshire council has, during his or her year of office, a project which raises money for a charity. Phil Barnett was Chairman for 2000/2001 and while seeking inspiration for his project he overheard two councillors discussing 'beating the bounds' of a local parish. The idea of 'the walk' was born. A walk around the boundary of West Berkshire met with widespread approval and Phil decided that any money raised would be used to support the Thames Valley and Chilterns Air Ambulance.

The walk

A programme of eight walks was planned and publicised with the help of footpath and support officers, parish councillors and West Berkshire Ramblers. Coffee and lunch stops were arranged in parish halls and a minibus organised to help walkers to get to the start of walks and then back to their cars. It was also necessary to have a back up vehicle for emergencies and for those whose enthusiasm was not matched by their stamina. Each of the walks was about twelve miles or so and transport was needed for those who would not make it to the end of each walk.

The first walk, which launched the project, started from Child Beale park on the third Sunday of September 2000. The press and the Air Ambulance were there to see off the walkers and about 60 people lined up for the photograph. This first walk set a pattern of coffee and lunch stops which the walkers greatly appreciated. At various halls, on each walk, hot drinks were provided by volunteers who selflessly gave up precious time on Sundays. At Farnborough the High Sheriff invited us into his house, once the home of John Betjeman, for coffee and biscuits and the lecture room at Sheep Drove Organic Farm provided a convenient and unusual place for lunch.

The weather was a constant cause for comment and concern. Mild and damp, warm and damp, heavy showers, wet under foot and heavy rain appear in all reports. Who was going to forget arriving at West Woodhay hall like 'drowned rats' at lunch time on walk four. However other comments of a lovely frosty day, reasonable weather, warmth of the day and spring had really arrived, present the other side of the weather picture.

The walks all had their own character coloured by the weather and incidents along the way. There was the memorable fall of one walker into the River Enbome (no harm done, just a wetting). Sophie, the Chairman's dog, acted heroically when faced with three vicious dogs. Real ale campaigners joined at the Swan Inn, Inkpen, with a collection for the Air Ambulance and the local TV was there to film us leaving in good order. The foot and mouth epidemic started just before walk seven which put the last two walks in jeopardy of postponement or cancellation. It was decided to complete the walk using only lanes and roads, disappointing, but preferable to leaving the project unfinished. In the event the road walking was 'not too bad'.

The final walk from Compton back to Purley village hall was on a fine, spring day. A spontaneous collection by parishioners took place at Streatley and there was a photographic session at the gates of Child Beale park which was still sealed off. At Purley the press and walkers gathered for Uri Geller and the Chairman's chain of office was under threat. A substantial cheque was presented to the Air Ambulance, with a promise of more to follow. As the party drew to a close the highs and lows were discussed and there was an opportunity to thank all those involved in the project.

Phil Barnett

The book

The walk had been successful and popular and walking around the perimeter of West Berkshire, which covers over half the acreage of Berkshire, had captured the imagination of many people. A book was the obvious way forward. The Council decided not to publish so West Berks Ramblers felt this should be their privilege and pleasure.

An interested group of Ramblers met to sort out the project. There was a route but it had been designed to visit the villages and to fit into Phil's year as Chairman. The first decision was that 'the walk' had to be the best that could be devised, especially as much of it passes through the North Wessex Area of Outstanding Beauty. This is why the route takes us into Hampshire to the south of Newbury and strays over the border into Wiltshire. Testing the route, writing instructions, sorting out photographs and public transport takes time but it is work that Ramblers really enjoy.

It is hoped that following the route of The Chairman's Walk gives pleasure to many.

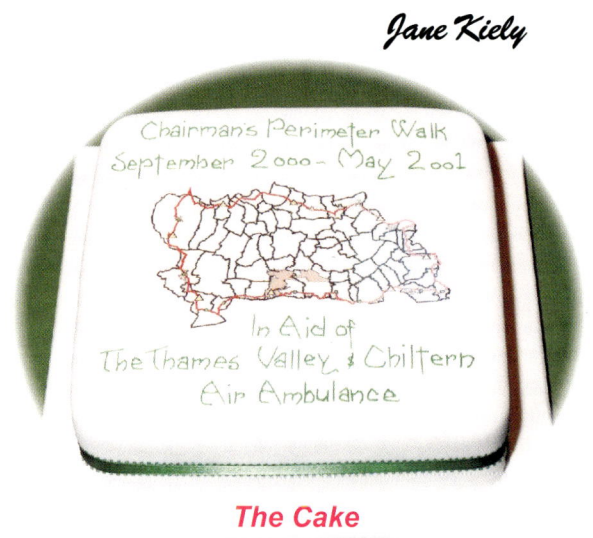

Jane Kiely

The Cake

GROUP MEMBERSHIP

Contact addresses for other Berkshire area groups are given below. Ramblers Association members may belong to whichever local group they wish to nominate and may receive the walks programme for another group on payment of a £2 annual charge sent to the Membership Secretary of the desired group. Cheques should be made payable to that group, e.g. 'East Berks RA', 'Mid-Berks RA', etc.

The Group Membership Secretaries (as at Sep. 2003) are:

EAST BERKS: Mrs Margaret Welch
Stoke Wood Cottage
Templewood Lane
STOKE POGES
Bucks
SL2 4AW

PANG VALLEY: Ms Jean Pitt
26 Queensway
Caversham Park Village
READING
Berks

MID-BERKS: Mrs Jean Hall
88 Corwen Road
READING
Berks
RG30 4SU

LODDON VALLEY: Mrs Barbara Curtis
39 Purfield Drive
WARGRAVE
Berks
RG10 8AR

WEST BERKS: Mrs Jean Bowman
4 Cansfield End
NEWBURY
Berks
RG14 1XH

GREAT PARK: Miss Pam Robinson
72 Dolphin Road
SLOUGH
Berks
SL1 1TA

SOUTH EAST BERKS:
John Moules
50 Qualitas
BRACKNELL
Berks
RG12 7QG

BERKSHIRE WALKERS:
(20's-30's group)
Caroline McDonagh
49 Sharnwood Drive
Calcot
READING
Berks
RG31 7YD

Acknowledgements

West Berks Ramblers have produced this book based on the original year 2000-2001 project of Councillor Phil Barnett, the then chairman of West Berks Council. All the routes can be found on O.S. Explorer maps 158, 159, 170, and 171 on which the maps in the book are based with the permission of The Controller of Her Majesty's Stationary Office, © Crown Copyright Licence No. MC 100028135.

Project Co-ordinator: Jane Kiely

Routes devised by: Ray Clayton, Patricia Cooper, Jane Kiely, Cliff Lambert, Neal Pike, Roy Steven, Geoff Vince and Fiona Walker.

Photographs by: Ray Clayton, Cliff Lambert, Neal Pike, Geoff Vince, Fiona Walker and Theresa Butler.

Maps and Graphics by: Geoff Vince

Public Transport Information researched by: Paul Frances

Published by: West Berks Ramblers

Printed by: Apple Print (01635 521654)

Our thanks go to everyone who has assisted with the original project and the preparation of this book, especially those who walked and checked the routes and directions.

WEST BERKS RAMBLERS is one of several groups across the region each of which arranges its own extensive programme of activities, short local and long distance walks and walking weekends. They can be contacted at 01635 32842 or at **www.wberksramblers.org.uk**. All the groups belong to the national organisation:

THE RAMBLERS ASSOCIATION, a registered charity which promotes country walking, protects rights of way, campaigns for access to open countryside and plays a major role in securing legislation to protect our paths and countryside.

As a member of The Ramblers you would be free to walk with any group and would be supporting this valuable work. If you would like to join us contact: **www.ramblers.org.uk**, telephone 020 7339 8501 or write to, The Ramblers Association, 2nd Floor, Camelford House, 87-90 Albert Embankment, London SE1 7TW.

Rights Of Way

There are over 100,000 miles of rights of way in England, some footpaths, some bridleways, some byways and some RUPPS, (Roads Used as Public Paths). Many of these date back to Roman times and beyond and most have an historic connection between villages or as coffin trails between outlying areas and churches. There is no doubt that the best way to see the countryside is on foot.

As well as finger posts most rights of way are marked with waymarks which, as well as indicating the route, use colour to show who may use the path, as shown below.

| Walkers only | Walkers, cyclists, horseriders | Walkers, cyclists, horseriders, motorcyclists and vehicles | For varied usage |

Key To Symbols Used On The Maps

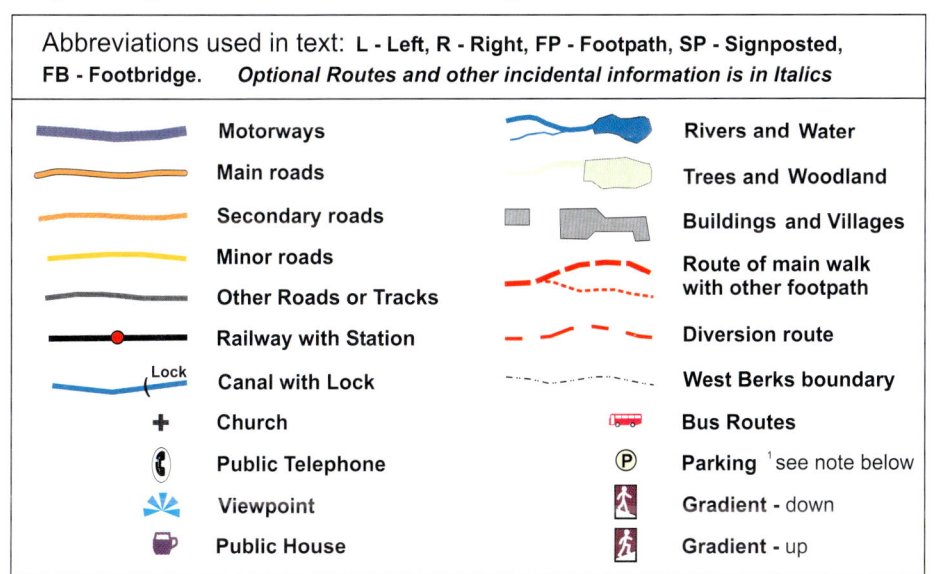

Abbreviations used in text: **L** - Left, **R** - Right, **FP** - Footpath, **SP** - Signposted, **FB** - Footbridge. *Optional Routes and other incidental information is in Italics*

Symbol	Meaning	Symbol	Meaning
	Motorways		Rivers and Water
	Main roads		Trees and Woodland
	Secondary roads		Buildings and Villages
	Minor roads		Route of main walk with other footpath
	Other Roads or Tracks		
	Railway with Station		Diversion route
	Canal with Lock		West Berks boundary
	Church		Bus Routes
	Public Telephone	P	Parking [1] see note below
	Viewpoint		Gradient - down
	Public House		Gradient - up

Please note: 1. This symbol shows a place where there is space to park. The safety, legality or advisability of parking there is for the driver to decide.

Public Transport

Public Transport can be used to reach the start and/or return from the finish of most of the walks and, in the case of bus services, other points on many of the walks. Seeing that all the walks are linear, public transport will be particularly useful in accomplishing the various sections/parts of these walks.

Trains

Thames Trains operates three local services from Reading as follows (useful intermediate stations shown in brackets):-

1) Bedwyn [Theale, Aldermaston, Midgham (Woolhampton), Thatcham, Newbury Racecourse, Newbury and Hungerford].
2) Oxford [Tilehurst, Pangbourne and Goring & Streatley].
3) Basingstoke [Mortimer and Bramley].

Most of the services to Bedwyn and Oxford originate from London Paddington and call at numerous stations en-route. Timetables are available from staffed stations, also times are posted at all stations, or telephone 08457 484950.

Buses

A complex network of bus services operates throughout the area covered by the walks. In rural areas buses will stop anywhere where it is safe to do so; just tell the driver when you want to get off or hail a bus if you wish to board. The walk maps indicate the bus services applicable and the table on the next page shows which company operates each service and their telephone number. Timetables may be obtained from libraries, tourist information offices and bus stations. West Berkshire Council has produced seven area public transport guides and any of these may be obtained by telephoning 01635 519663. Likewise Wiltshire County Council can supply timetables of services operating in their county and they have a "Bus Enquiry Line" - telephone 08457 090899. There is also a national public transport information service known as "Traveline" and they may be contacted during quite extensive hours by telephoning 0870 608 2608.

Bus Services	Operators	Telephone Nos
1,20*,20A*,32A,44A,123,124	Stagecoach in Hampshire	01256 464 501
3A,3B,3C,6,9,13,32,101,102,103,104	Newbury Buses	01635 567 500
18,25,30,31,33,38,44,45,143,148,149	Reading Buses	0118 959 4000
20#,20A#,22,22A,X20	Wilts and Dorset	01722 336 855
46,47	Thamesdown Transport	01793 428 428
73,99,99A,107,114	Four Valleys Taxibus	01635 358 06
74,113(To Newbury),120,X48	Weavaway Travel	01635 820 028
113(To Combe)	Burghfield Mini Coaches	0118 959 0719
82	Barnes Coaches	01672 540 330
84,85	Royal Mail Postbus	01635 370 97
132,142	Thames Travel	01491 837 988
154	Horseman Coaches	0118 975 3811
N1	Heyfordian Travel Ltd.	01869 241500
X2,X22	Harley Travel	01672 512 786
RCB	Ramsbury Community Bus	01672 520 555
ST	Stewarts of Mortimer	0118 933 2221

* For walks 4a, 4b, 4c.
\# For walks 5a, 5b, 6a.

The production of this book has been assisted by a grant from:

waste recycling environmental

WREN

waste recycling GROUP PLC

Funding the future with Waste Recycling Group's Landfill Tax Credits

Section 1

Pangbourne to Burghfield Bridge

Part 1a

Part 1a - Pangbourne to Little Heath - About 7km (4.5ml)

Section 1 of the Chairman's walk starts in Pangbourne where there are 4 car parks, a railway station, public toilets, telephones and shops. The route leaves Pangbourne along an attractive section of the Thames Path to Mapledurham Lock then gently rises through fields and woods to the west of Tilehurst before dropping down into the Kennet Valley. It then crosses the Holybrook and the railway line to end along a rural section of the River Kennet/Kennet and Avon Canal.

1. To start the walk go down Whitchurch Rd. To join the Thames path at the Adventure Dolphin Centre. Turn R to walk downstream with the river on your L to reach Mapledurham Lock.

2. Immediately after leaving the lock turn R away from river through field to reach narrow lane with houses on L and recreation ground on R. At end of lane go R to Purley Village and where the road turns sharp L up hill, (Purley Lane), take FP on R until it emerges near railway bridge on L. Cross bridge and go uphill to reach A329.

3. Turn R for few metres then carefully cross A329 to enter Beech Rd and follow up hill and round to R. Continue until it bends downhill to R and take FP uphill ahead to reach field. Turn L and follow LH field margin around to R to cross open field ahead towards woodland. At wood turn L and follow field edge with wood on R, soon continuing on straight path through middle of field to a cross track.

4. Continue ahead towards farm buildings at Stoneham Farm. At road turn R to follow narrow, winding road *(take great care)* for about 100m. *(It is possible to walk inside the wood, parallel to the rd., to cross a small ditch opposite the Mud House)* Take care crossing the end of Long Lane and enter FP to L of Mud House.

Continue on 1b

Pangbourne to Burghfield Bridge   _Section 1_
Part 1b

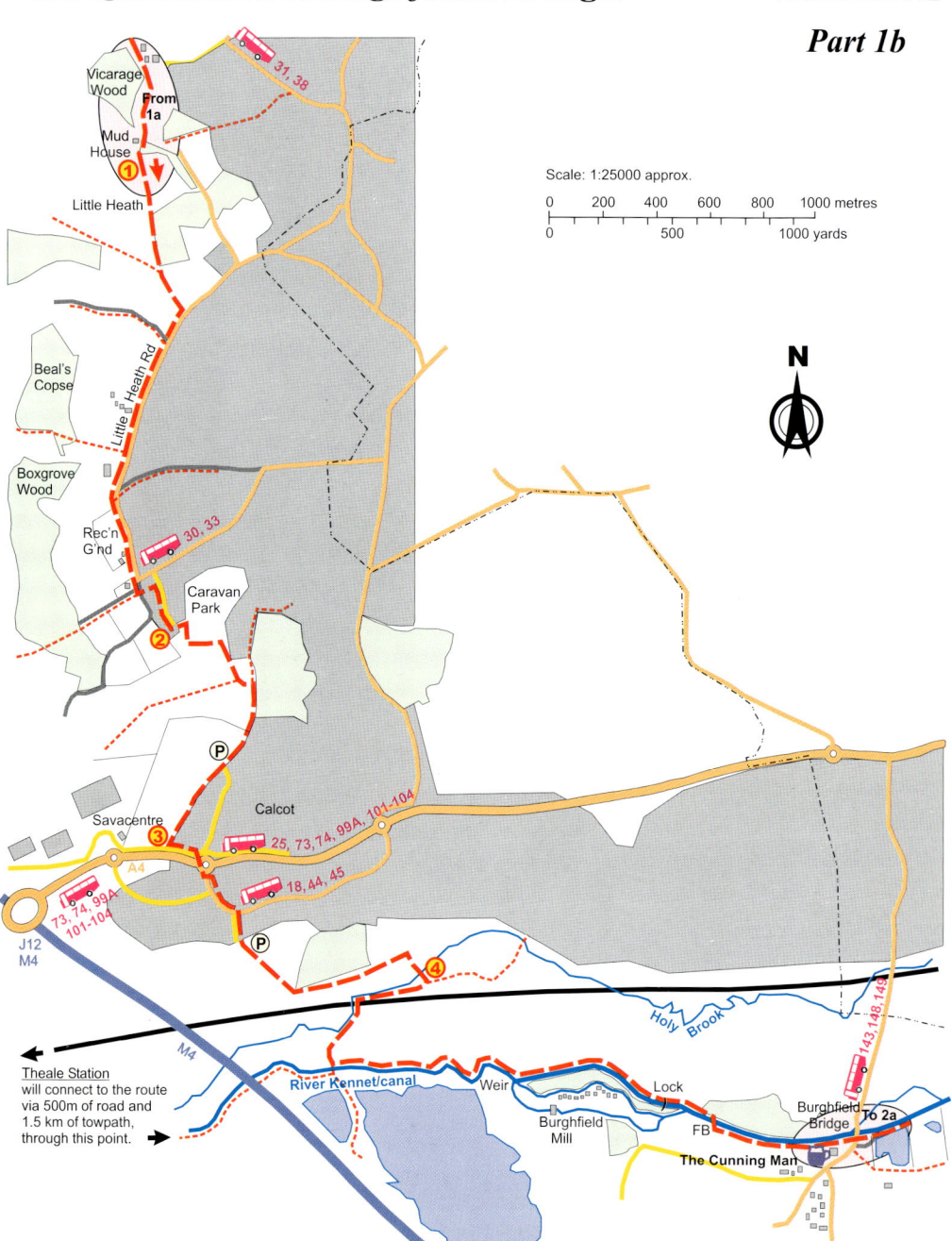

Part 1b - Little Heath to Burghfield Bridge - About 7km (4.5ml)

1. Follow path from the Mud House. It curves L to reach Little Heath Road. Turn R along road to reach the recreation ground. At junction with City Road go ahead on tarmac FP, parallel with and to L of Pincents Lane, between a brick wall and hedge. At end of FP turn L into Cowslip Close then R along Farm Drive.

2. Continue ahead past Barley Walk. At end of road turn L to take grassy track on R, opposite house number 55, through rough ground, emerging at top of field through iron kissing gate. Take FP to L along top of field, first parallel with mobile homes then following field edge downhill to go through kissing gate on L. Pass through safety barrier, down steep slope to second barrier near houses on L. Turn R and continue down hill, through car park of Calcot Centre and down L side of recreation ground to main A4 road.

3. Turn L along small side road then cross A4 at controlled crossing just before roundabout.
At roundabout turn R into Charrington Rd then 2nd R into Rushmoor Gardens to emerge into recreation ground. Go half L, around football area to small post at end of spinney to the rear of Beansheaf Community Centre where two culverts meet. Turn L and follow grassy track between trees on L and marshy area on R. Shortly after end of marshy area turn R over culvert and follow track round the L side of copse to cross bridge over Holy Brook.

4. Immediately turn R to follow grassy track towards railway with Holy Brook on R. **Cross railway with extreme caution** and go ahead along RH field margin to bridge over River Kennet/canal. Do **NOT** cross bridge but turn L along path with river/canal on R. Shortly after passing Burghfield weir and lock cross FB over river/canal, turn L and follow towpath to car park at Cunning Man.

(The old Cunning Man was demolished whilst this book was being prepared. It is has been re-built and these pictures show the old and the new).

Continue on 2a

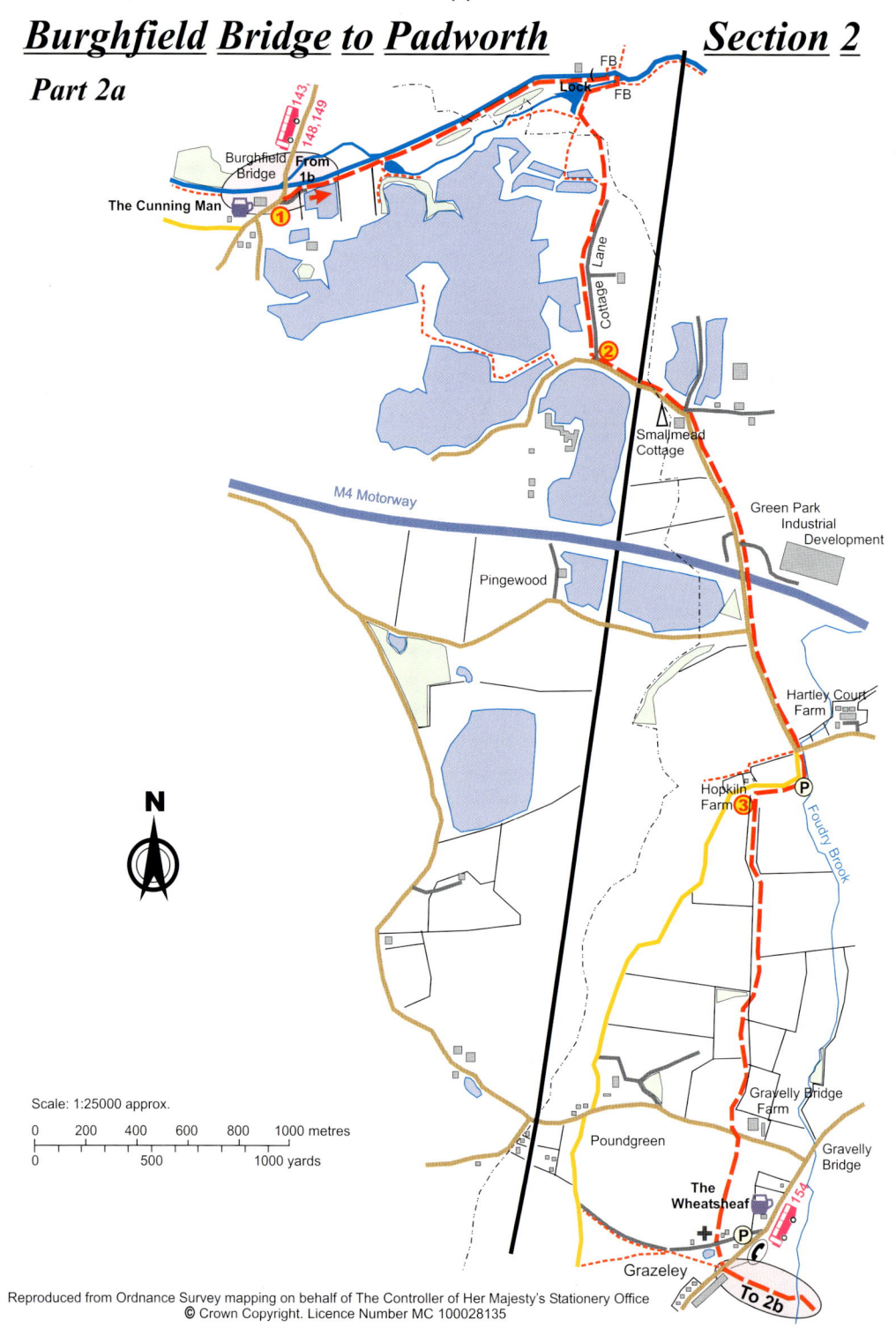

Burghfield Bridge to Padworth Section 2
Part 2a

14

Part 2a - Burghfield Bridge to Grazeley - About 6km (3.75ml)

The first part of this section is not the most picturesque passing, as it does, through an area of urban and industrial development and, of necessity, walking about 2km of road. Once off the roads however it improves considerably using quiet paths and green lanes which, at the right time of year and right time of day are full of the smell of honeysuckle, the sound of birdsong and the sight of deer, rabbits and other wildlife.

Parking was previously possible, by arrangement with the manager, in the pub car park. During production of this book however the old Cunning Man pub was demolished. It is currently being rebuilt and should be completed by the time this book is printed. Parking may be possible on the towpath access track but please ensure that access for wide vehicles remains possible.

Most of the extensive lakes along the Kennet valley are the result of gravel extraction, which still continues. Once extraction is finished many of the lakes are turned to leisure use. They also provide a valuable environmental resource with many birds, mammals and invertebrates living and breeding in the area.

1. Go down the access track to the towpath and turn R,(east), to follow the towpath for about 1km (3/4ml) to pass the lock. At the path end cross the FB on the R and turn R on the FP. Follow river and edge of first field to small stream. Bear half L on a FP across second field, through 2 lines of trees to turn R and follow path to a fishermen's car park. Follow Cottage Lane to the Pingewood road.

2. Turn L and follow the road over the railway and M4 continuing past the turning on R to Pingewood. Where the road turns L continue ahead on to a lane that bends R after about 100m.

3. 200m after the bend, opposite Hopkiln Farm, turn L to follow a waymarked FP for about 1.5km (1ml), initially between fields, then on the RH field boundary, bearing R to LH field boundary as shown on the map and keeping R at 'farm' gate. Cross a road by Gravelly Bridge Farm and continue ahead on another FP that crosses a field then leads down a path into Grazeley Churchyard and thence to a lane. Cross the lane into a recreation field keeping to the RH boundary to an opening on to a road.

Cross the road to follow a track by a school.

Continue on part 2b.

Burghfield Bridge to Padworth

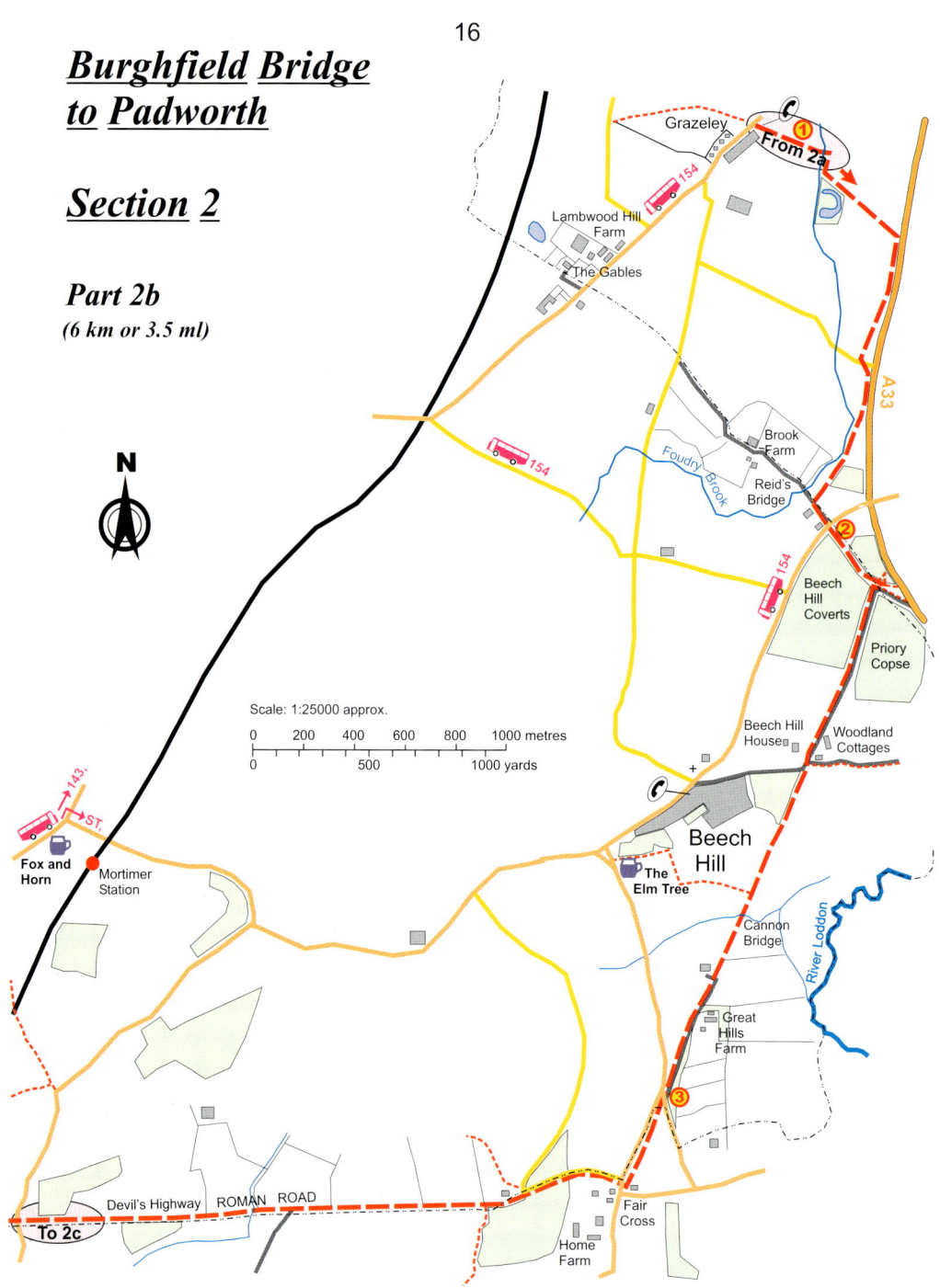

Section 2

Part 2b
(6 km or 3.5 ml)

Part 2b - Grazeley to Devil's Highway. About 6km (3.75ml)

Parking may be possible in Grazely recreation ground or, by arrangement with the landlord, at The Wheatsheaf.

3. Cross the road and continue up the road opposite. At the staggered junction turn R and where the road bends sharply R continue ahead down a track - the Devil's Highway - following the line of a Roman road which once went to the Roman town of Calleva Atrebatum at Silchester. Continue on this track, passing an area where it is deeply rutted and almost destroyed by off-road vehicles, to meet a road.

Continue on part 2c.

1. Continue down the track from section 1 to a foot bridge and turn R to follow a field edge path around by a copse then on a crossfield path heading towards the A33 road. Turn R to follow a path that runs adjacent to the A33 to a road junction with a cattle grid. Cross the road to a path opposite which continues alongside the A33 for a while before bearing R and meeting a track leading to Brook Farm.

2. Turn L onto the track to meet a road. Cross the road and follow a clear track through the woods ahead. At a junction of paths go ahead then immediately R over a wooden bridge then R again at the tarmac road. Follow this quiet lane to pass a barrier, some houses and a junction on the L then, as the lane bends R, bear L down an unsurfaced track. After 1km (0.5 ml) the track becomes surfaced again and meets a road.

Burghfield Bridge to Padworth

Section 2
Part 2c

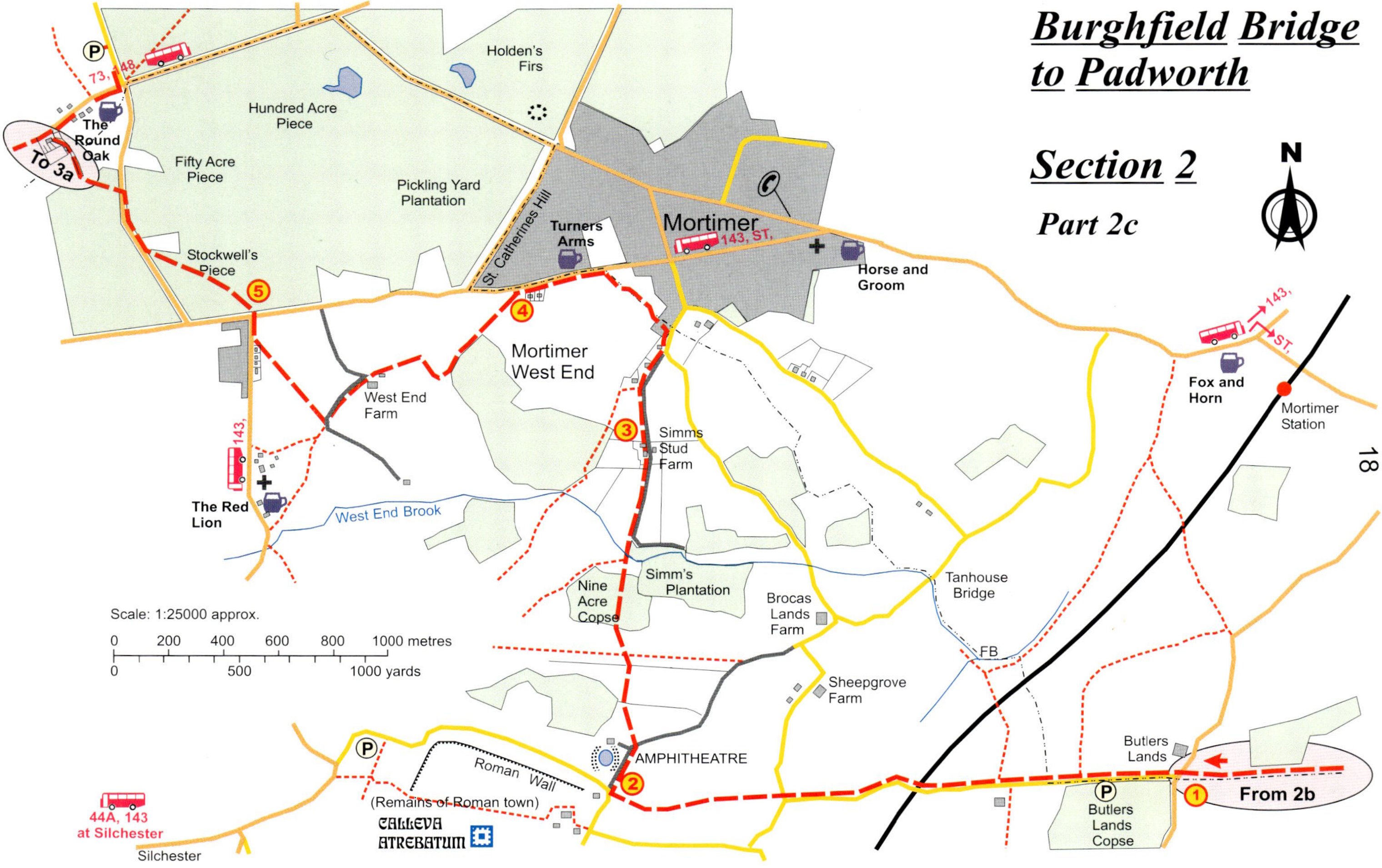

18

Part 2c - The Devil's Highway to Padworth. About 7km (4.5ml)

Parking is possible in several laybys by Butlers Lands Copse, at the Roman Remains and at Silver Lane near the end of the walk.

1. Cross the road and continue down the lane opposite. Stay on this lane to cross the railway and come to a junction. Take the FP opposite across the fields to emerge on a road at a finger post.

To divert and visit the remains of Calleva Atrebatum, the Roman Town at Silchester, either continue along the road ahead or turn L for about 100m then R along a farm track.
To continue the walk turn R down the lane leading past the Amphitheatre.

2. Follow the lane for about 200m and as it narrows and bends R turn L through a V stile. This FP heads across the field towards nearest pylon to cross a stile. Continue ½ R up hill to a second stile beside gate then ¼ L across another field to enter Nine Acre Copse. Follow the path that winds down through the copse, across a water meadow (keep R at the fence) and West End Brook and head uphill again within the hedgerow, to Simms Stud Farm.

3. At the farm the path widens to a track and later becomes a tarmac lane. Another lane joins from the R. Immediately after the second house on the L, 'Bosket', take the FP on the L. Cross a stile to walk to the L of a hedge before bearing R through the hedge to follow the path with the hedge now on your L then bear L again just before meeting West End Road in Mortimer. Turn L and using the pavement on the opposite side pass the Turners Arms and a small row of houses on the L to turn L just past the last house and join a track bearing ½ R.

4. The track runs between two fields then leads downhill with woodland on the L. As this ends turn R onto another track which turns ¼ L by a pylon and heads up to West End Farm. At the farm junction bear L and after about 100m, at a tarmac cross roads, take a track to the R which leads to Church Road. Turn R for a few paces to meet Chapel Road. Cross carefully to the FP opposite.

5. Follow the FP, bearing slightly L, until it meets Ramptons Lane. Just before the lane turn R onto an unofficial path running alongside the lane and watch for a FP going off to the L from the lane. Follow this path to Padworth Road.
(To access the car park in Silver Lane turn R then L at the cross roads.) If continuing the walk, turn L for about 100m.

Continued on 3a

Padworth to Greenham Common   Section 3

Part 3a

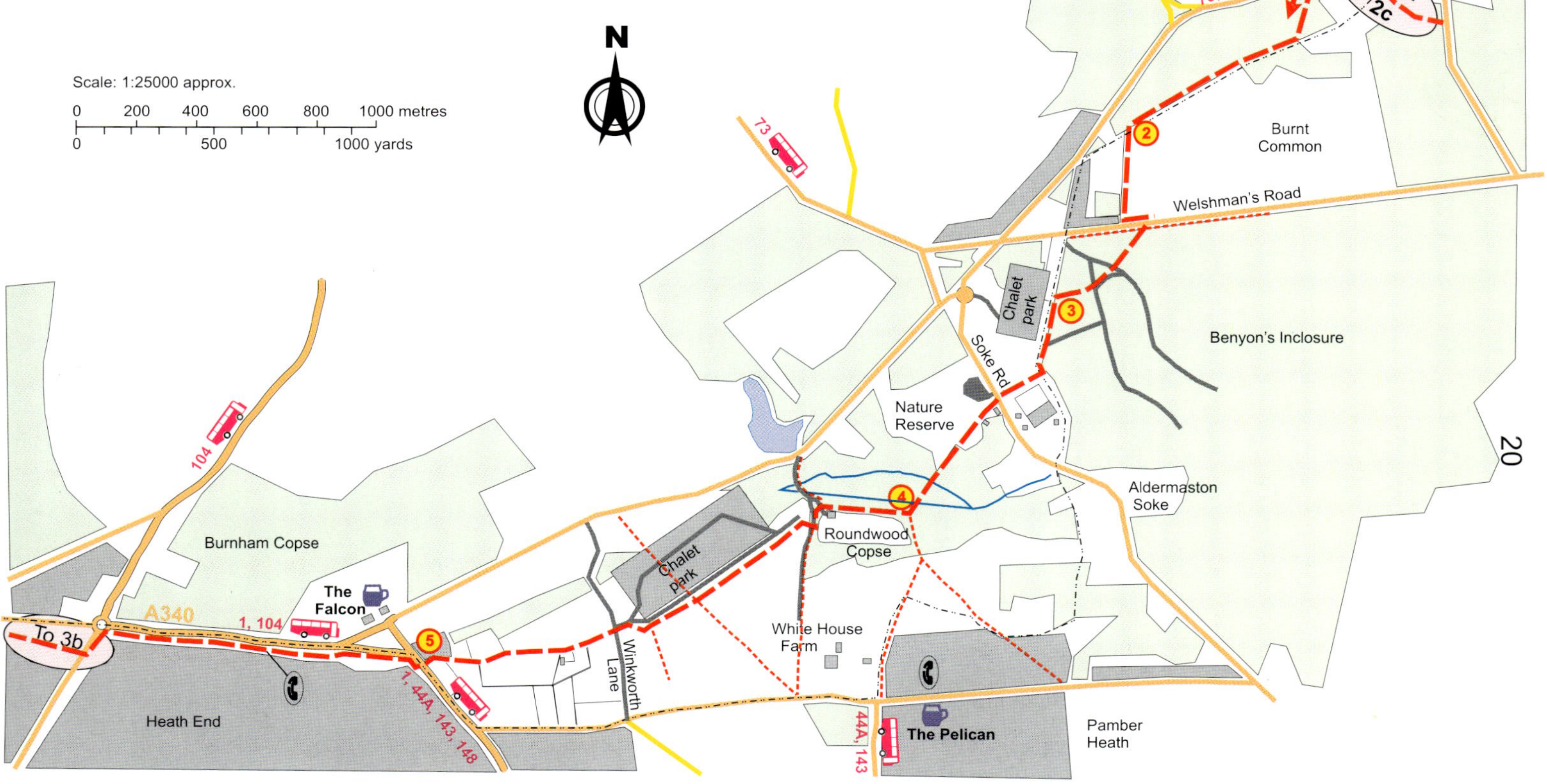

Part 3a - Padworth Common to Tadley - About 6km (3.75ml)

Section 3 covers an attractive area with a wide variety of countryside on offer from woodland riverside to wide open heathland, water meadows and agricultural fields. There is a variety of footpaths, bridleways and tracks and the freedom to choose your own paths through common land and a nature reserve. The West Berks boundary is with North Hampshire and parts of the walk are on the Hampshire side.

<u>Parking</u> is possible 150m down Silver Lane.

If starting from the car park - walk up to Padworth Rd and turn R. Pass the Round Oak pub and the first FP on the L then:

1. Turn L onto the next FP heading through woodland. Cross a path to a house on your L and as the path forks, bear L across a common, over a FB and a stile. Turn R through a wooded area before crossing a stile and following the field edge. Pass to the R of some earthworks to bend L then R at the end.

2. After some new tree planting turn L to follow a green path to Welshman's Rd. *(Note, this path is diverted from the position marked on the OS map).* Just before the road cross a V stile to the L and follow the FP on the LH side of the hedgerow. After a short distance turn R over a V stile and FB to cross the road onto FP opposite. Turn R then immediately L onto grassy track for 100m. Cross a gravel track to a short path then turn R on next grassy track. Follow this to cross a gravel track and continue to meet a path alongside the chalet park.

3. Turn L on this path, continuing past the end of the chalet park for 200m to turn R through a chicane gate. Ignore the FP L and go ahead on to the common then bear ½ L. Just past some gates on L, bear L on to a path that leads to Soke Rd. Turn L then R down track immediately after the entrance to Decoy Heath nature reserve. This soon becomes a path and descends through woodland in to a valley, over a FB and up the other side.

4. At the top is a SP junction. Turn R to follow wood edge to road by Keepers Cottage. Turn R downhill then after 50m turn L on FP to briefly join track then bear R on FP again for 30m. As chalet park comes into view bear L at waymark for 60m, cross path and go through kissing gate. Turn R then L on path beside chalet park road. At end go through 2 gates on to road and turn L. Cross Winkworth Lane and follow the byway to meet Mulfords Hill Rd, (A340).

5. Cross the road and turn R for a short way to 'The Triangle'. Turn L and shortly you will see a service road on the L running parallel to the A340. Follow the grassy strip between the two roads to reach Heath End Rd. By a roundabout.

Continued on 3b

Padworth to Greenham Common   Section 3 Part 3b

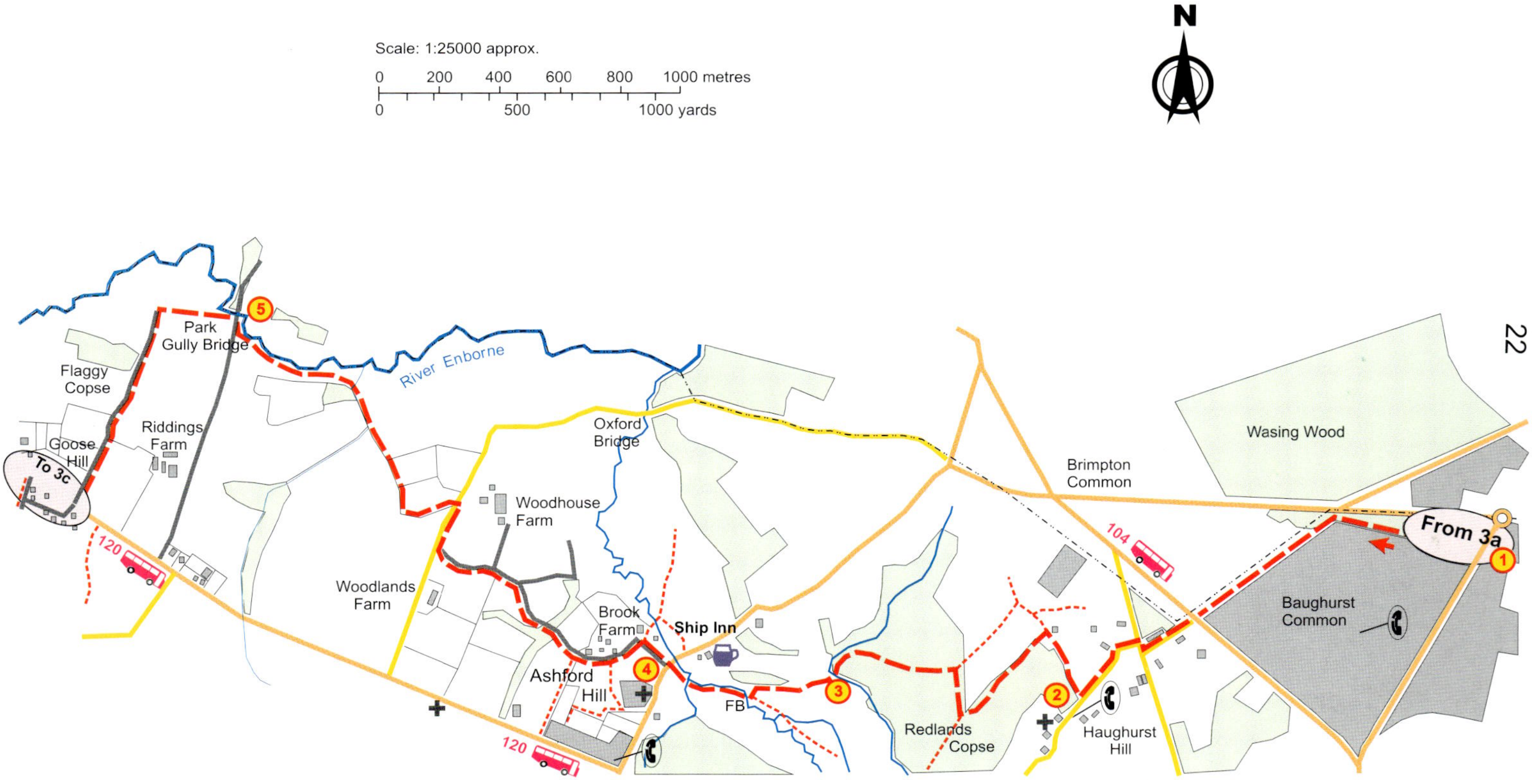

Part 3b - Tadley to Goose Hill - About 6km (3.75ml)

1. By the roundabout cross Heath End Rd. and turn L to follow the fencing on the R until it ends by the county sign. Cross the fence on the R to follow a local path running through woodland to a FP going off to the L. Follow this over a hillock keeping L by garages then straight ahead, following the County boundary past Baughurst Common School on the L. Cross Brimpton Rd and go down the lane opposite which meets another road. Turn R then immediately L down Haughurst Hill Rd to about 50m before the 'phone box to turn R onto a FP.

2. Follow this down into a valley then up to turn L at the top through a rather scruffy vehicle yard. This leads to a very attractive path through Redlands Copse. Where this meets a path turn R up the slope, parallel to the field fence. Just before reaching a gate on the R turn L onto a path. Ignore the private path going L and continue down to a stile.

3. Cross the stile into the Nature Reserve and bear a little R across the water meadow to a kissing gate. Cross the next field to a stile and FB. Turn R and keep to R side of the meadow with the stream on the R to go through a kissing gate and onto the road at Ashford Hill close to the Ship Inn; *(just up the road to the R)*

Through the copse turn L and follow the path alongside the River Enborne to where it meets the concreted Riddings Lane.

4. Take the gravel path opposite, Old Lane, up to Brook Farm where it goes L then bends around to the R. Where the track continues up to a cottage and the path forks L, take the path until it meets a tarmac lane. Turn R on the lane then after about 150m turn L onto a FP. This field side path turns R after a short distance and leads down to a copse.

5. Turn R then L onto a path before the metal 'Park Gully' bridge. The path turns away from the Enborne across a field then turns L again into the middle of an attractive hedgerow called Park Lane. This meets a track for a short while then goes back into a hedgerow and heads up to Ashford Hill Road in Goose Hill. Turn R onto the road for about 500m.

Continued on 3c

Padworth to Greenham Common Section 3 Part 3c

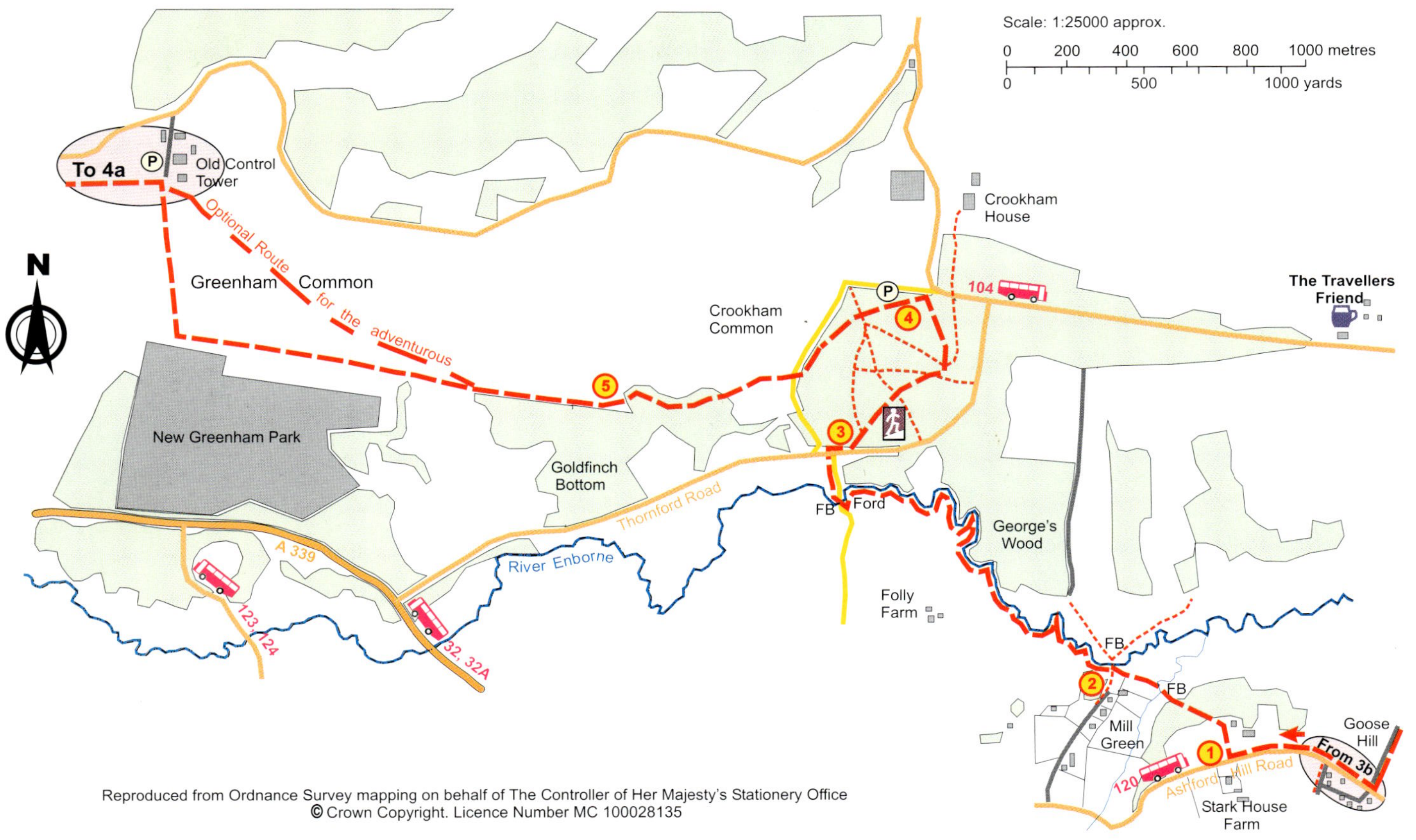

Part 3c - Goose Hill to Greenham Common - About 5.5km (3.5ml)

1. After about 500m, immediately past Stark House Farm on the L, turn R onto a FP. At the bottom of the field this track turns L then R away at a fork turn R onto a smaller path. Follow this down through Stoneylands Copse *(full of bluebells in season)*, cross a small FB over a stream and head slightly R towards the River Enborne. At the end of the field turn L over a FB then keep the hedge on the L to reach a stile.

2. Cross the stile and turn R towards a FB over the Enborne. Don't cross the bridge but take the path along the L bank of the river. The path follows the meandering Enborne for 2½ km (1.5ml) passing a cottage with a mill wheel on the opposite bank then a weir. After the weir the river widens and the path emerges onto a road with a ford on the R. Cross the river by the FB past the ford then follow the road to reach the busy Thornford Road. Turn R onto a FP. Turn R and cross the road carefully to a FP.

3. Follow the path up a steepish hill to go straight on at a crossing path at the top. Follow the posts marked with a purple flash. Soon a path merges from the L so bear half R to follow the new direction. When you see the path ahead leading to a gate turn L onto a smaller path. This leads to a car park at Crookham Common, *(containing a large map of Greenham and Crookham Commons)*.

4. Turn L in the car park to leave by another path at the W end still marked with the purple marking posts and with the road a short distance to your R. After a while the purple path leaves to the L but continue ahead, now on the blue route. Cross a gravel track and continue to meet the road that was on your R. Opposite is a gate in the stock fencing surrounding Greenham Common. Pass through the gate and follow the path ahead until it meets the main E - W path by a copse on your L. Continue on the blue route passing the copse then turning sharply L down into the woods where it turns R to eventually emerge back onto the common.

5. Turn L onto the path which hugs the trees to the L and eventually re-joins the main E-W path by New Greenham Park, an industrial area on the L. Pass a large concrete pillar *(impressive - but just a marker between Greenham and Crookham commons)* and **either** turn half R and find your own way across the common to the control tower, **or** continue along the fence and at the marker post turn R, go over the runway cross and follow the track to the control tower and main car park.

Continued on part 4a.

Greenham Common to Walbury Hill   Section 4   Part 4a

Part 4a - Greenham Common to Wash Water - About 7km (4.5ml)

Section 4 leaves the common at Greenham to pass along the footpaths, bridleways and quiet residential roads on the borders of NW Hampshire, eventually climbing to join the Wayfarers' Walk. This long distance path provides magnificent views as it takes us across Walbury Hill, an ancient iron age fort and the highest point in Berkshire. Here we leave it to go NW whilst the Wayfarers' Walk becomes the Test Way and heads South.

1. Leave the car park walking towards the common past the control tower. Turn R along the path running in front of the control tower and continue, following orange posts, until it ends at a junction. Turn R leading to the NW gate and out into a small car park. Turn immediately L and through a gate onto a tarmac FP which leads around the W end of the common in a loop. Just after the tarmac ends turn R on a major crossing path, eventually passing a fence on the L, to a fork. Take the signposted path to the R into woodland, through a gate, across a field, bearing slightly L, and over a stile to the A339(T) Basingstoke Road. Go R 20m.

2. Cross road to finger post. Go over stile and follow track along L side to far corner of field. Up the steps, turn L. At Swan Inn fork L onto Newtown and Burghclere road passing church on R. Climb the hill to take woodland footpath to R at 'Woodcote'. Ignore L turns. At T junction turn R, go over bridge and at gate turn R to continue through wood to reach stile. Keep woodland to R and go to stile in corner of field at far end of tennis court. Go straight ahead to reach Apple Tree Cottage on R. Continue ahead to cross (A339) road to finger post.

3. Follow track and after 40m turn right. Follow gravel lane towards buildings. Pass between houses, Ivy Cottage on R, Jubilee cottage on L, continuing downhill, through gate and bear R to follow footpath along edge of field with Fence on L. Cross 2 stiles and bridge over stream. Continue down R side of next field to stile. Follow L edge of three fields to reach wood. Follow track until tarmac lane is sighted on R. At gate bear L then immediately R to follow FP parallel to lane to stile. Continue along edge of field to further stile to join lane. Go ahead to reach the A343.

Continue on 4b

Greenham Common to Walbury Hill   Section 4   Part 4b

Part 4b - Wash Water to Heath End - About 6km (3.75ml)

1. Cross road and follow track to reach stile to R of house. Follow path to reach road at Enborne Row. Turn L and pass under A34 bridge. Take the first turning L and at end of bend in road go L through gate into The Chase, (National Trust) then immediately R to follow track, parallel with road, to car park.

2. Take main path from car park. After 50 metres, by first big tree, turn R onto grassy path. Follow through trees, turning L then R at fence to reach road. Cross road and take lane opposite. Turn L onto road and then R at T junction to bottom of hill. Turn L onto bridleway, initially beside stream, and follow to meet track. Bear R then turn R at road.

3. After passing first open field on L turn L onto bridleway which is metalled; *(Ignore "No Access" sign)* Follow R then L around buildings and just after row of 3 garages turn L to pass corrugated iron barn. Follow track and veer R to cross stile beside metal gate

4. Enter field at sign post and bear half R across field passing to R of mound near far hedge to cross stile. Continue direction across next field towards first large tree in RH hedge and cross stile. Head for far R corner of small field to cross stile. Follow path between fence and hedge to road. Turn L and then bear R onto East Woodhay road for about 100 metres. Cross stile on R and take footpath that bears half L.

Continue on 4c

Greenham Common to Walbury Hill

Section 4   Part 4c

Part 4c - Heath End to Walbury Hill - About 5.5km (3.5ml)

1. Follow the line of the L hand waymark across field to gap in hedge. Maintain line through next field passing L of water trough to reach stile beside metal gate. Follow fence of cottage to stile in far corner of field. Turn L into sunken lane and follow to reach the green at East Woodhay. *(Note church and fine house - 'Old Rectory')* Turn R onto minor road towards West Woodhay. Keep straight on at joining road then, after passing Berries Farm entrance, turn L onto bridleway. **(For alternative route to avoid very steep hill see 2a at end.)**

2. Go ahead onto green lane, later becoming attractive, hedged path. Go through gate at far end then head straight up very steep hillside. Go through metal gate above tree line and continue climb over brow of hill, aiming slightly R, to exit through farm gate. Turn R onto 'Wayfarer's Walk' *(also known as the Southern Ridgeway)*. At road turn L then R at T junction. At next bend go straight ahead onto track to continue following Wayfarer's Walk over top of Walbury Hill, *(Ancient Monument - Iron Age Hillfort)*, to reach car park on western side.

2.a *(Alternative route to avoid very steep hill.)* Do not take bridleway to L, continue on road, turn L onto road signed 'Faccombe'. Ignore bridleway crossing road and continue up hill to footpath on R. Follow direction of sign to reach far R hand corner of wood then uphill in same direction to metal gate. Cross road, turn R onto Wayfarer's Walk.

Continue on 5a

Walbury Hill to Hungerford

Section 5

Part 5a

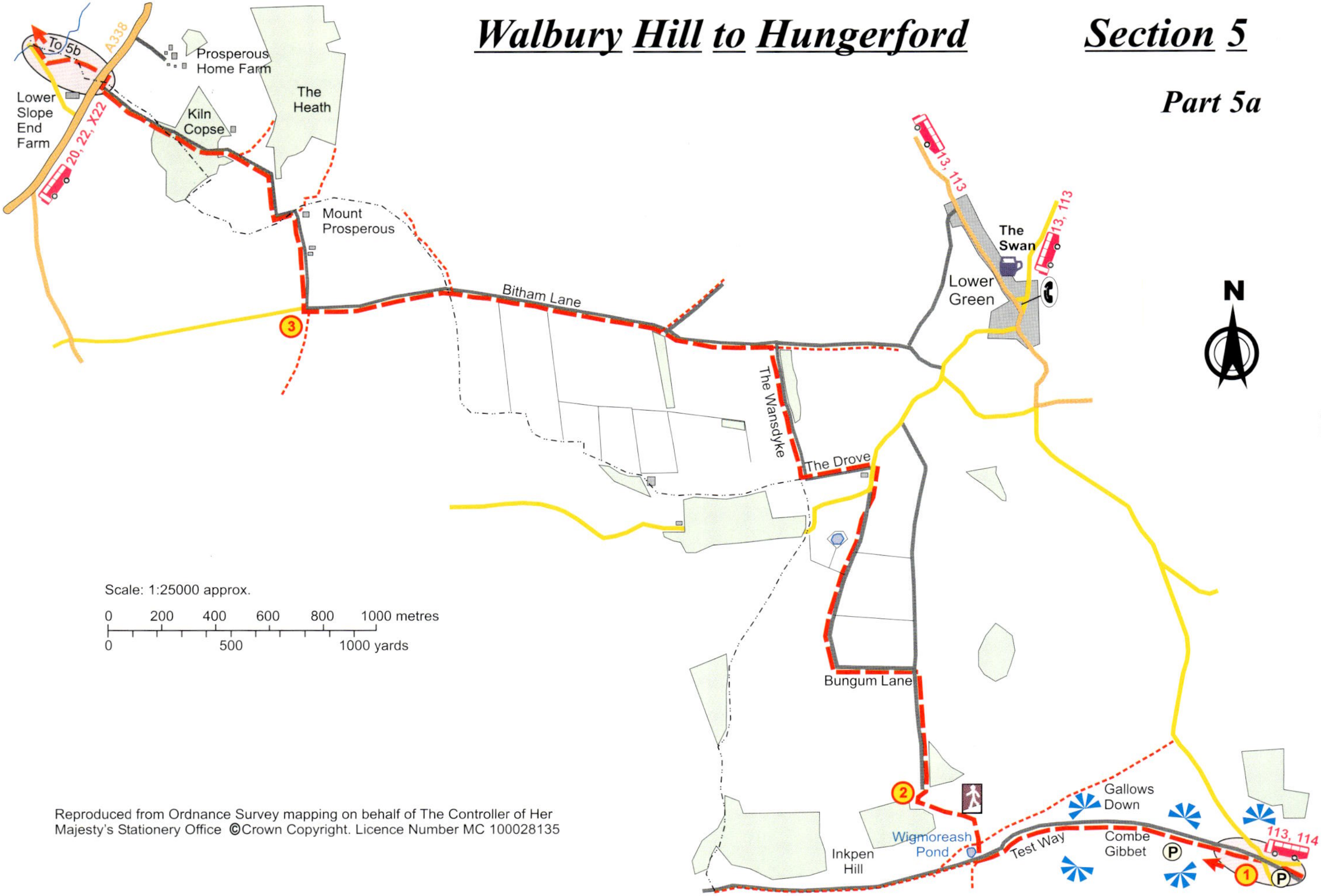

Reproduced from Ordnance Survey mapping on behalf of The Controller of Her Majesty's Stationery Office ©Crown Copyright. Licence Number MC 100028135

Part 5a - Walbury Hill to Lower Slope End Farm - About 7km (4.5ml)

This section of the walk starts high on the downs where, on a clear day, there are exceptional far reaching views. Here also can be seen the famous Combe Gibbet where, after a hanging at Winchester gaol, bodies were left to hang as an example to others. The route carries on through an ancient drovers track (Bitham Lane) and passes through some delightful working countryside until, at low level, the Kennet and Avon canal is reached where the peace and tranquillity of barging may be observed.

1. From the car park head W towards the Gibbet and continue to Wigmoreash Pond, (concealed to R). Before FP junction turn diagonally R through gate and after 50m head down the steep slope until grassy track is reached. Turn diagonally L and continue to bottom of hill bearing R before trees.

2. Continue between hedgerows turning L into field (Bungum Lane) and R at far end between hedgerows until the road is reached. Keep foward and then turn L past a cottage and then R and uphill to continue until Bitham Lane is reached. Turn L and continue forward to the tarmac road, (about 2km or 1mile).

3. Turn R and head for Mount Prosperous. Turn L at T junction and follow road, continue over cattle grid and leave track through gate on L in edge of wood to follow the footpath and emerge onto the main A338 road.
Cross road (with care), turn R then L through gap in hedge and follow path, bearing slightly L, following stiles across fields.

Continue on 5b

Walbury Hill to Hungerford — Section 5

Part 5b

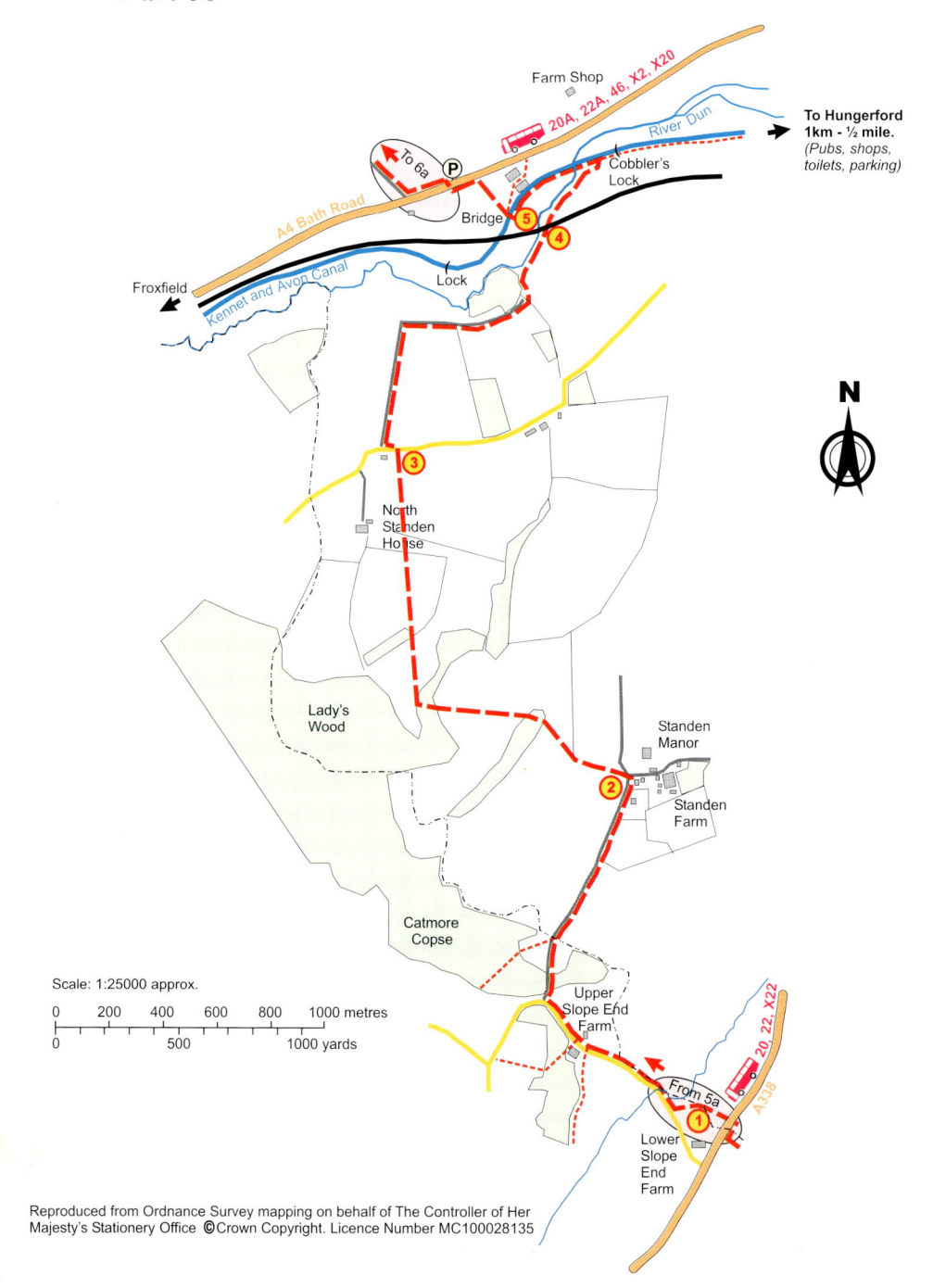

Part 5b - Lower Slope End Farm to Hungerford - about 6km (3.75 ml)

1. From field path exit onto road. Turn R and continue along road passing Upper Slope End Farm, then turn R at cottage. Follow the track until the post box at Standen Manor is reached.

2. Turn L and follow the path past farm buildings and continue in the direction of the electricity line/poles. After emerging from the wood turn R then diagonally R along recently diverted path, *(this will vary from the public right of way shown on the older OS maps)*, through the metal gate to again follow the electricity lines/poles until a road is reached.

3. Cross road to continue along path, bear R to walk track between hedgerows where, at bottom, turn R until emerging into a field where the LH edge is taken until a stile in the fence is reached.

4. Climb stile and go up and over the railway line and over another stile. Turn R and follow LH border to pass over stile and emerge onto the canal towpath at Cobbler's Lock. Turn L towards Froxfield.

5. Cross stepped wooden bridge over the canal and walk uphill to follow permitted path *(not shown on OS map)* to the A4 main road. Turn L along footway until opposite layby and then cross the road (with care). Continue along road After 100m turn R between hedgerows to follow a track.

Continue on 6a

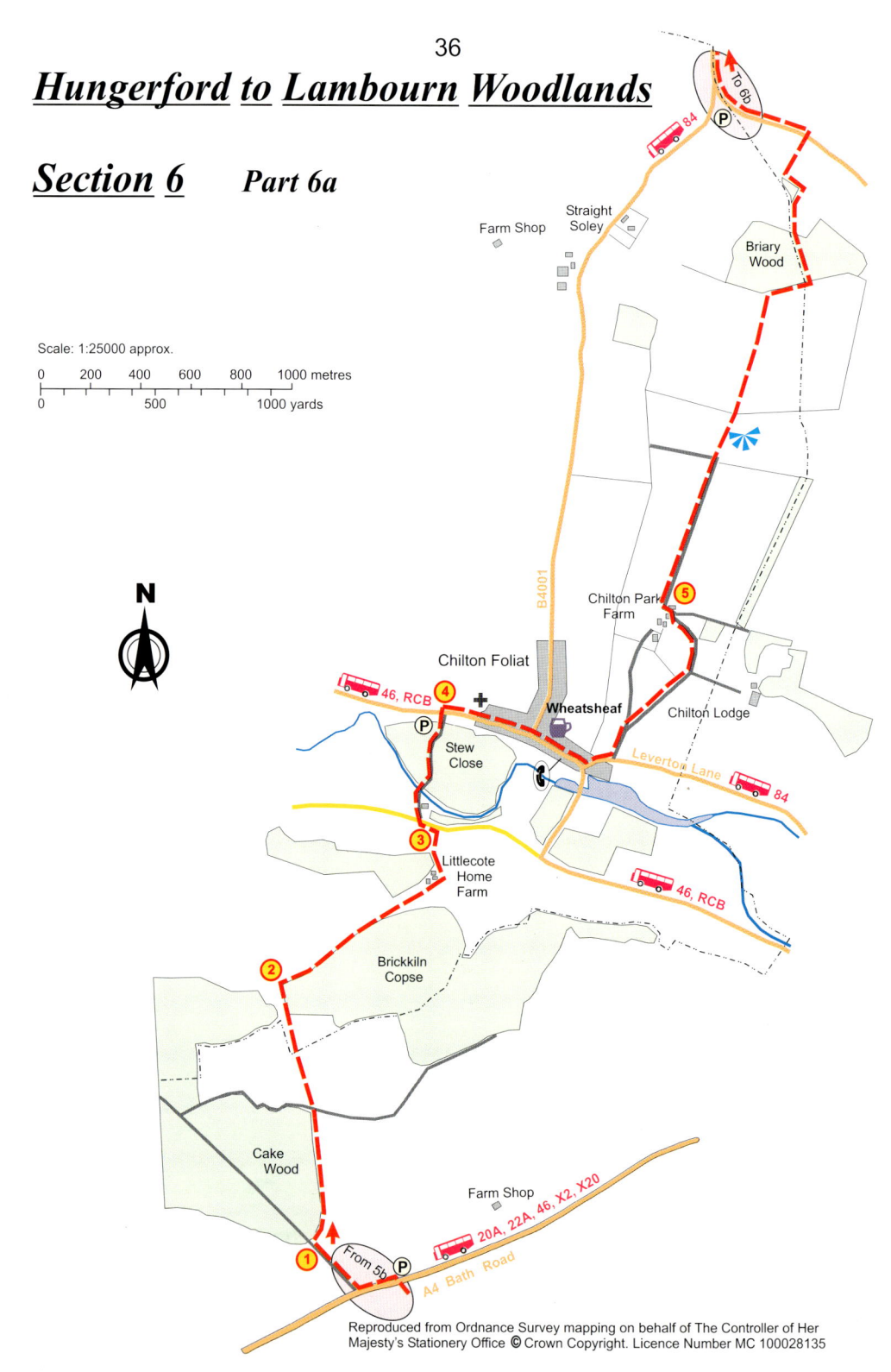

Hungerford to Lambourn Woodlands

Section 6   Part 6a

Part 6a - Hungerford to Straight Soley - about 7km (4.5ml)

A varied, interesting and undulating walk through rural countryside and woodland; some historic buildings and good views along much of the route.

1. Follow the track from the A4. After about 250m bear R. Keep Cake Wood on L until open field is reached. Cross field in same direction and slightly to the R of the marked dip in the tree tops ahead to a path in the gap on the edge of Brickkiln Copse.

2. Keep wood on the R and follow track along edge of the wood until an old farm building is reached. Turn L and head down to the road.

3. Turn L along road and take FP R for Chilton Foliat, crossing the River Kennet by long wooden bridge and passing through Stew Close Wood to emerge on pavement. Turn R

4. Head East through Chilton Foliat *[Church and a variety of old buildings]*. At far side of village fork L onto Leverton Lane for few metres, then take L turn onto driveway to Chilton Lodge. Follow drive up slope; at FP sign keep R, still continuing to climb. Where drive divides for the Lodge *['historic' house 1800s, but hardly visible from path]*, take L fork towards Chilton Park Farm. At top of drive keep L to pass tithe barn and flint house.

5. Turn R to follow gently ascending track towards Briary Wood. On reaching trees, turn R to follow headland path alongside wood. After short distance turn L at FP sign to enter the wood. Follow broad track through wood then, just before trees end, veer L at waymark sign onto narrow path to exit the wood. Continue straight ahead along field edge keeping hedge on L at all times. Turn L at corner of field, R at next corner, then follow headland path down to meet lane at Old Hayward Bottom. Turn L to follow lane (or adjacent grass strip) to Y junction with the B4001. Fork R onto road **(N.B. THIS CAN BE BUSY)**.

Continued on 6b

38

Hungerford *to* *Lambourn Woodlands*

Section 6   *Part 6b*

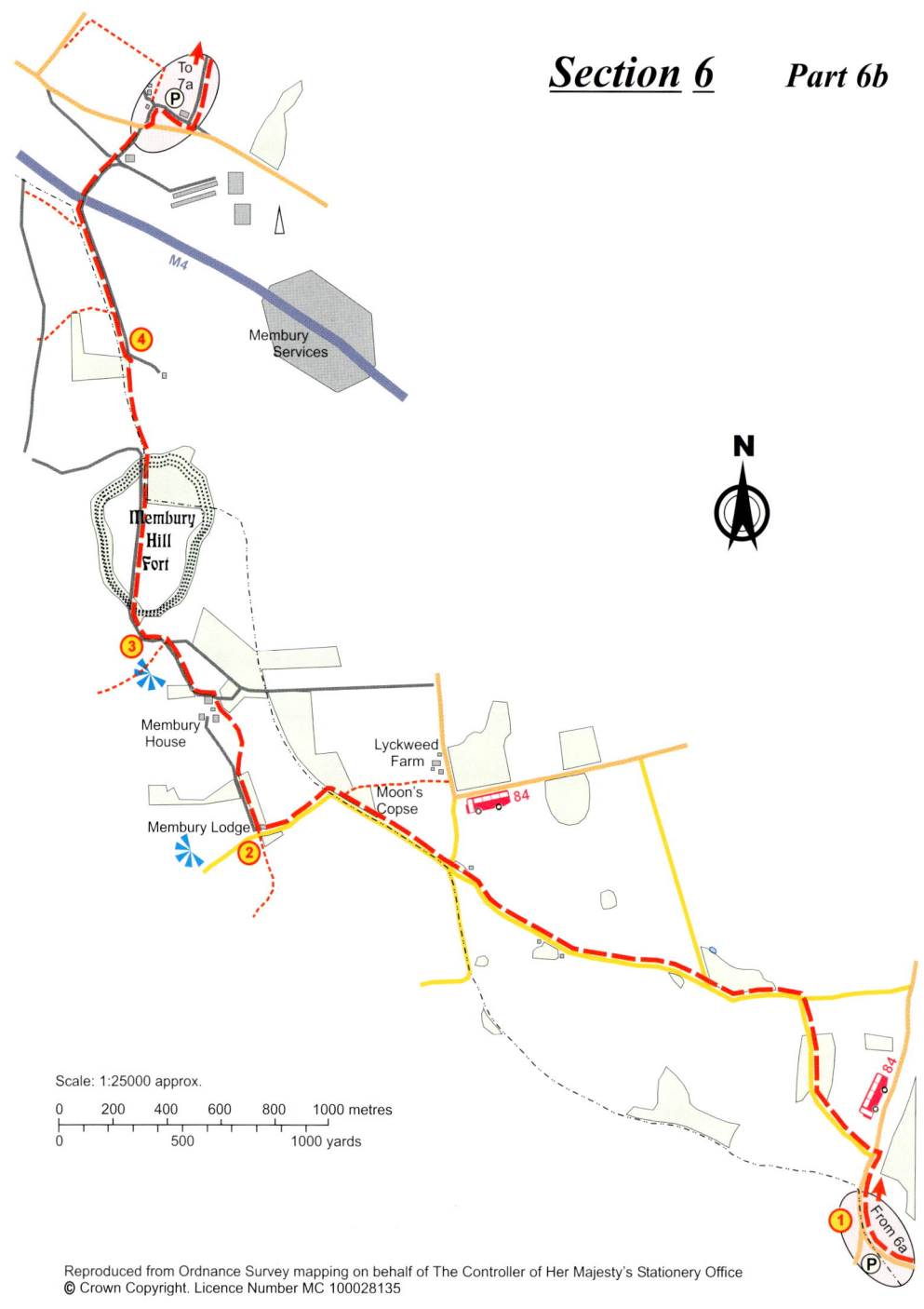

Part 6b - Straight Soley to Lambourn Woodlands - about 6.5km (4ml)

1. Follow B4001 for few yards, then take next L turn signposted 'Bearfield Lane'. Follow narrow, rough surfaced track uphill to T junction; turn L, then keep straight on to follow high level lane for 800m (3/4 mile) before descending to staggered junction of minor lanes. Cross straight over onto lane signposted 'Membury'; follow this past Moon's Copse and around sharp LH bend to reach Membury Lodge.

2. Turn R through gates (small gate is unlocked) to follow Right of Way along driveway to Membury House. Take R fork where drive divides; continue on through grounds, keeping buildings to L *[Note - Clock tower in old stable block]*. At yard head half L between barns aiming for far corner. Turn R through gates. Continue straight ahead on rough track around rim of hillside. Bear L at joining track and keep straight on through farm gate to enter wooded area at top of Hill Fort.

3. Follow track as it bends R, then turn L at T to cut through the earthworks, across the centre of the Hill Fort, and then exit at far side through earthworks again before descending towards field. Keep straight ahead along R.H. edge of field, keeping hedge on R, to reach small wood. Follow narrow path through edge of trees, cross stile at far side and bear R up slope to meet stony track.

4. Turn L, following track Northwards to pass smelly pit and on towards the motorway. Cross footbridge over M4, pass to L of house to reach main road *[Roman road- Ermine Street]*. Cross over straight onto track (which was the "Old road"), and follow round R past cottages to reach old metal barn on L.

Continued on 7a

40

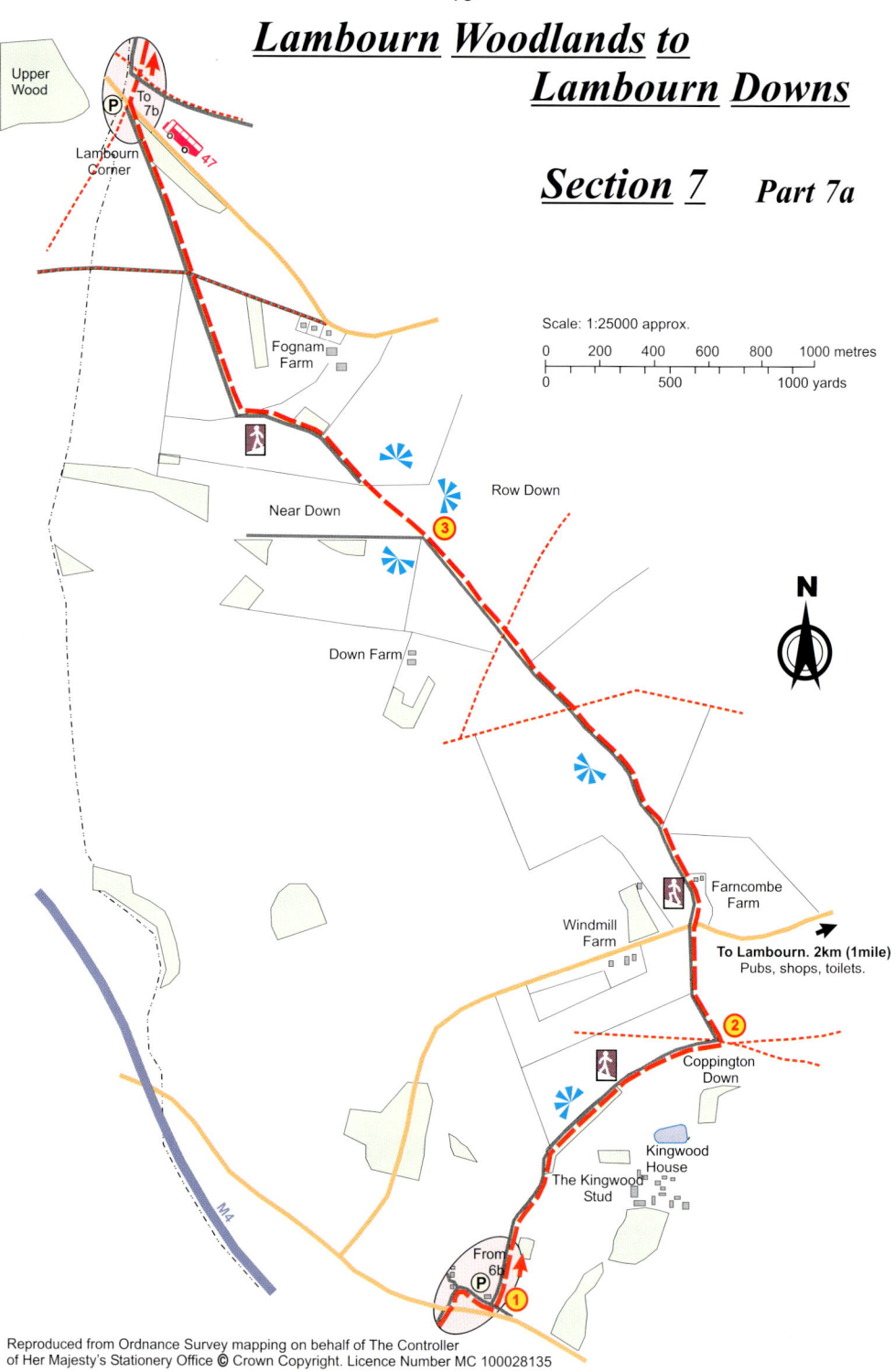

Lambourn Woodlands to Lambourn Downs

Section 7   *Part 7a*

Scale: 1:25000 approx.

0   200   400   600   800   1000 metres
0   500   1000 yards

Upper Wood

To 7b

Lambourn Corner

47

Fognam Farm

Row Down

Near Down

Down Farm

Farncombe Farm

Windmill Farm

To Lambourn. 2km (1mile)
Pubs, shops, toilets.

Coppington Down

Kingwood House

The Kingwood Stud

From 6b

M4

N

Reproduced from Ordnance Survey mapping on behalf of The Controller of Her Majesty's Stationery Office © Crown Copyright. Licence Number MC 100028135

Part 7a - Lambourn Woodlands to Lambourn Corner - About 6km (3.75 ml)

A hilly, downland walk; wide open spaces and wonderful views.

2. At crossing paths turn L onto byway (NOT FP on L, check map) which leads up to Baydon Road. Cross straight over to continue on byway. Follow past Farncombe Farm and up rise. Keep straight on at next two crossing tracks gradually ascending all the time over the Downs.

1. From the 'Old Road' turn L alongside the barn onto bridleway. Follow this level path for short distance before descending steeply to foot of Coppington hill.

3. At the top of down leave track to veer slightly R across gallops. At far side join stony track and follow downhill for about 2km (1ml) to meet road (B4000) at Lambourn Corner. Bear R across road to join chalk track.

Continued on 7b

Lambourn Woodlands to Lambourn Downs   Section 7   Part 7b

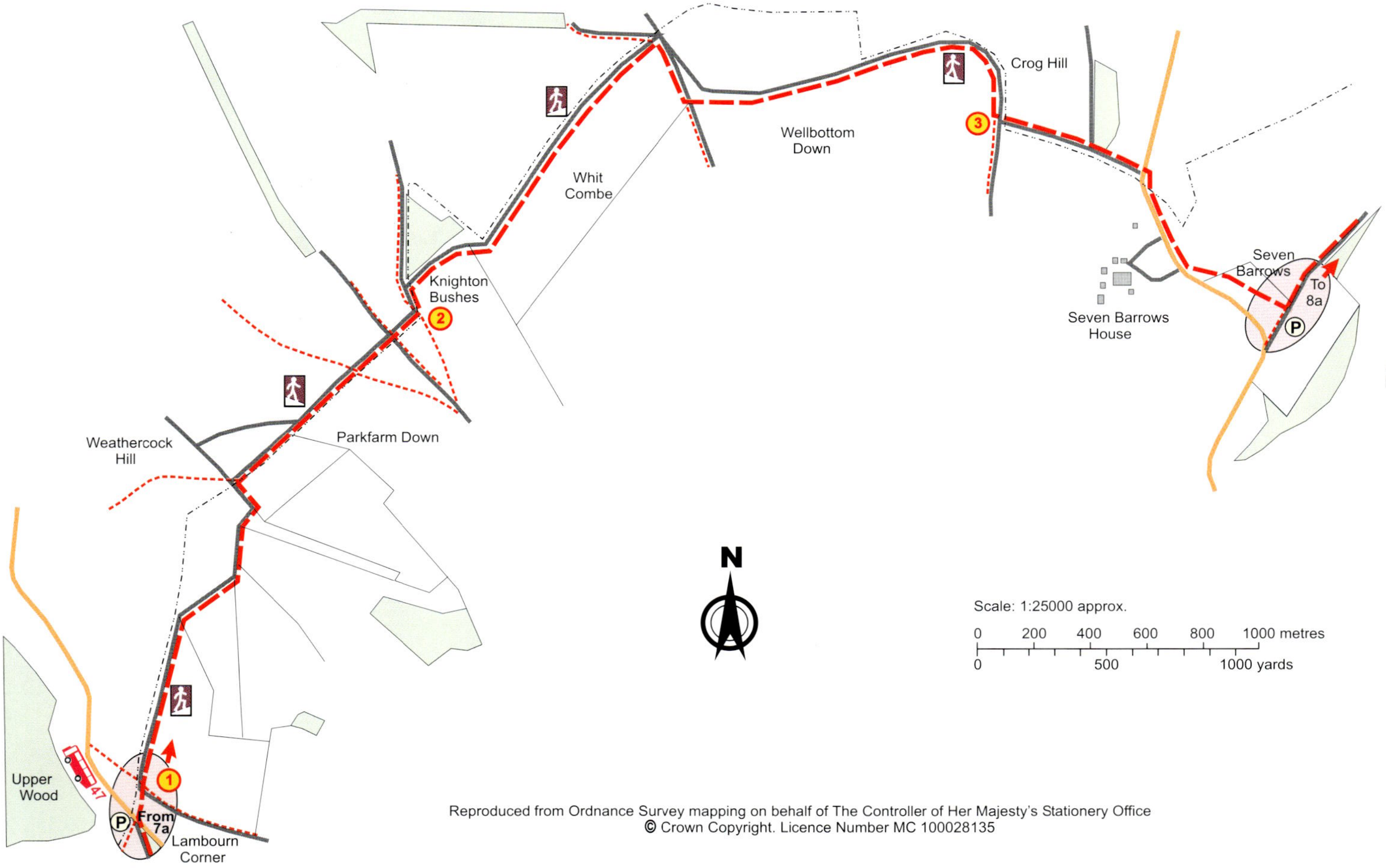

42

Part 7b - Lambourn Corner to Seven Barrows - about 6.5km (4ml)

1. Follow chalk track which climbs the Eastern side of Weathercock Hill. At top keep following track round to L with fence on R to reach ROW signpost and crossing path. Turn R to follow stony track descending Parkfarm Down. Keep straight on at crossing byway.

2. At field edge bear L to follow track towards Knighton Bushes. At edge of wood turn R onto grassy track which climbs up Whit Coombe onto Wellbottom Down. At top immediately turn R and follow path between railings. Where LH fencing ends turn L and follow gently descending grass track for just over 1Km (3/4 mile) bending round to R at foot of hill.

3. At waymark post turn L then follow grass track past Beech Copse to exit at road. Turn R along road. After passing 2nd driveway cross road to go through gap in fencing to enter Seven Barrows Nature Reserve, *(dogs under control please)*. Turn R keeping hedge on R and walk across rough grass to reach small parking area.

Continued on 8a

Lambourn Downs to Fawley Section 8

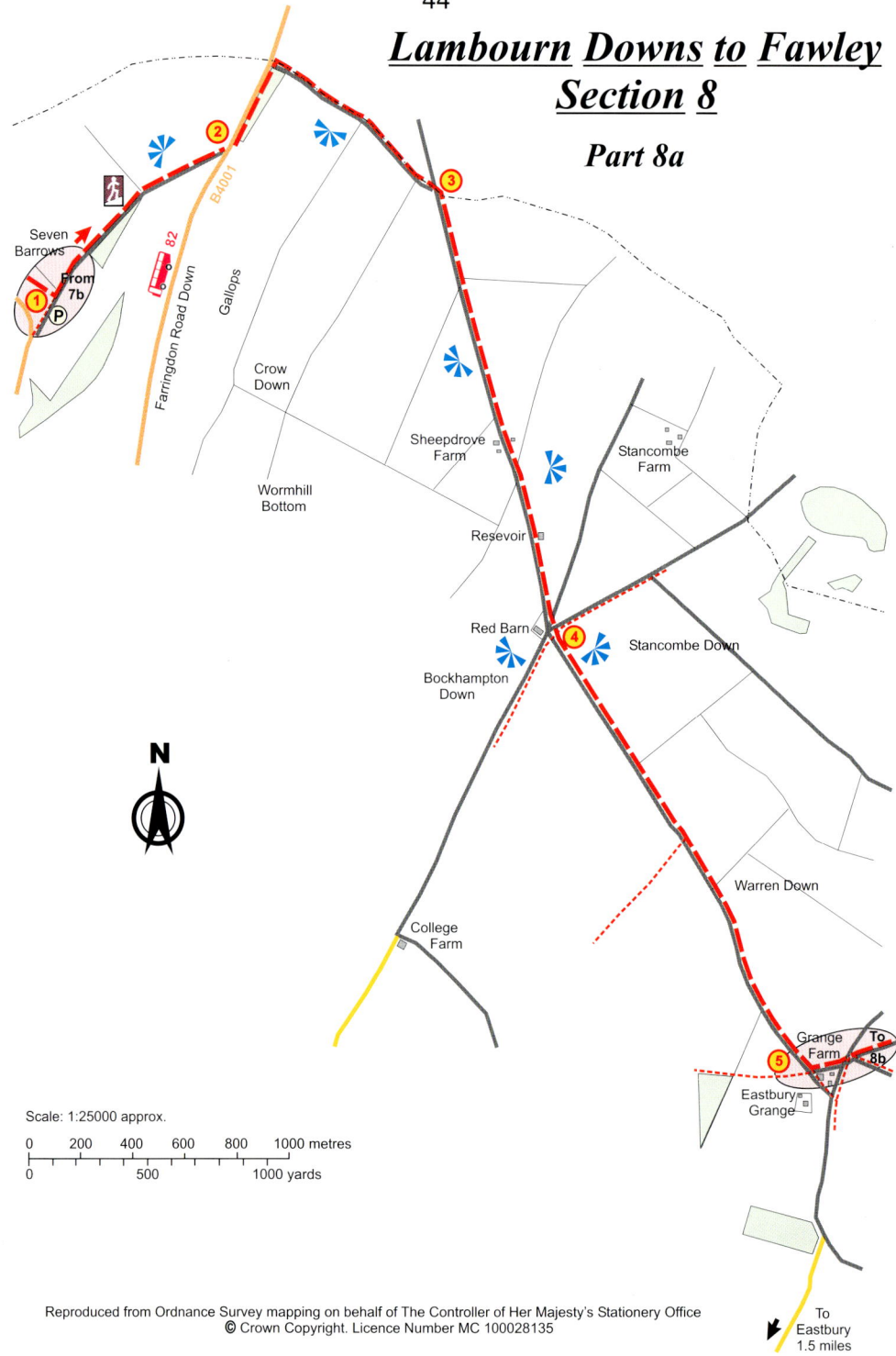

Part 8a

Part 8a - Seven Barrows to Grange Farm - About 5km (3ml)

Section 8 of the Chairman's Walk takes you across open downland passing places with such evocative names as 'Crow Down'', 'Wormhill Bottom' and 'Old Warren' to pass through the tiny Downland village of Fawley. We hope you don't meet too many 'off roaders' to spoil your enjoyment.

1. From the Nature Reserve car park at Seven Barrows head NE up track through copse, past gallops and through small copse to road.

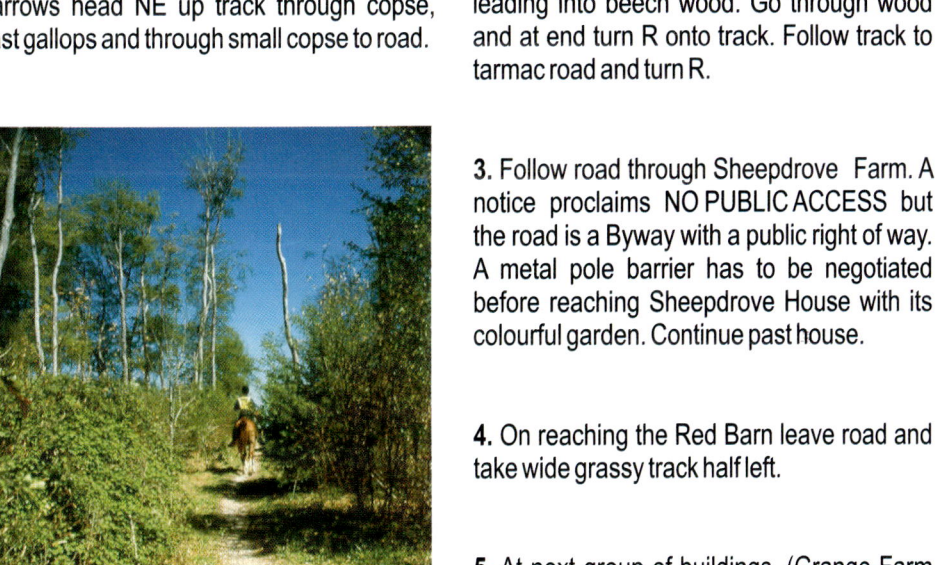

2. Cross road and bear L on narrow path leading into beech wood. Go through wood and at end turn R onto track. Follow track to tarmac road and turn R.

3. Follow road through Sheepdrove Farm. A notice proclaims NO PUBLIC ACCESS but the road is a Byway with a public right of way. A metal pole barrier has to be negotiated before reaching Sheepdrove House with its colourful garden. Continue past house.

4. On reaching the Red Barn leave road and take wide grassy track half left.

5. At next group of buildings, (Grange Farm but not named on ground), turn L. Ignore signpost after 50m but at next one (a further 50m) keep L on lower track. View to left is perhaps marred by movable hen houses, *(but at least not battery hens)*

Continued on 8b

Lambourn Downs to Fawley   Section 8   Part 8b

46

Scale: 1:25000 approx.

Part 8b - Grange Farm to Fawley Monument - About 5km (3ml)

1. Keeping to the lower path pass one cross track (bridle path) and at top of hill, where there is another, keep straight on down wide earth track.

2. Turn L on metalled road to Old Warren. Follow road around house and then, where it turns sharp left, turn R on to path at RH side of field fence.

3. Follow path through hedge and L around field edge. At top of field turn L over stile (which looks like a seat). At steel gate keep to RH side of fence along grassy track to road, which leads down to Fawley church.

Roadside parking only in Fawley.

4. With church on your L, continue down the road through Fawley. *(Just before the telephone box on the left there are some steps to a small wrought iron gate which is the old churchyard for the original church for Fawley and South Fawley and as a millennium project the villagers are trying to find the grave of Thomas Hardy's grandmother.)* Continue down the road to T junction, cross carefully over the main A338 (Wantage road) and over stile, bearing slightly R, to follow sunken track to top of hill. Go through squeeze stile and continue in same direction across the gallops ahead. Follow line of gallop fence to bottom of field and stile.

Continued on 9a

Fawley to Compton   Section 9   Part 9a

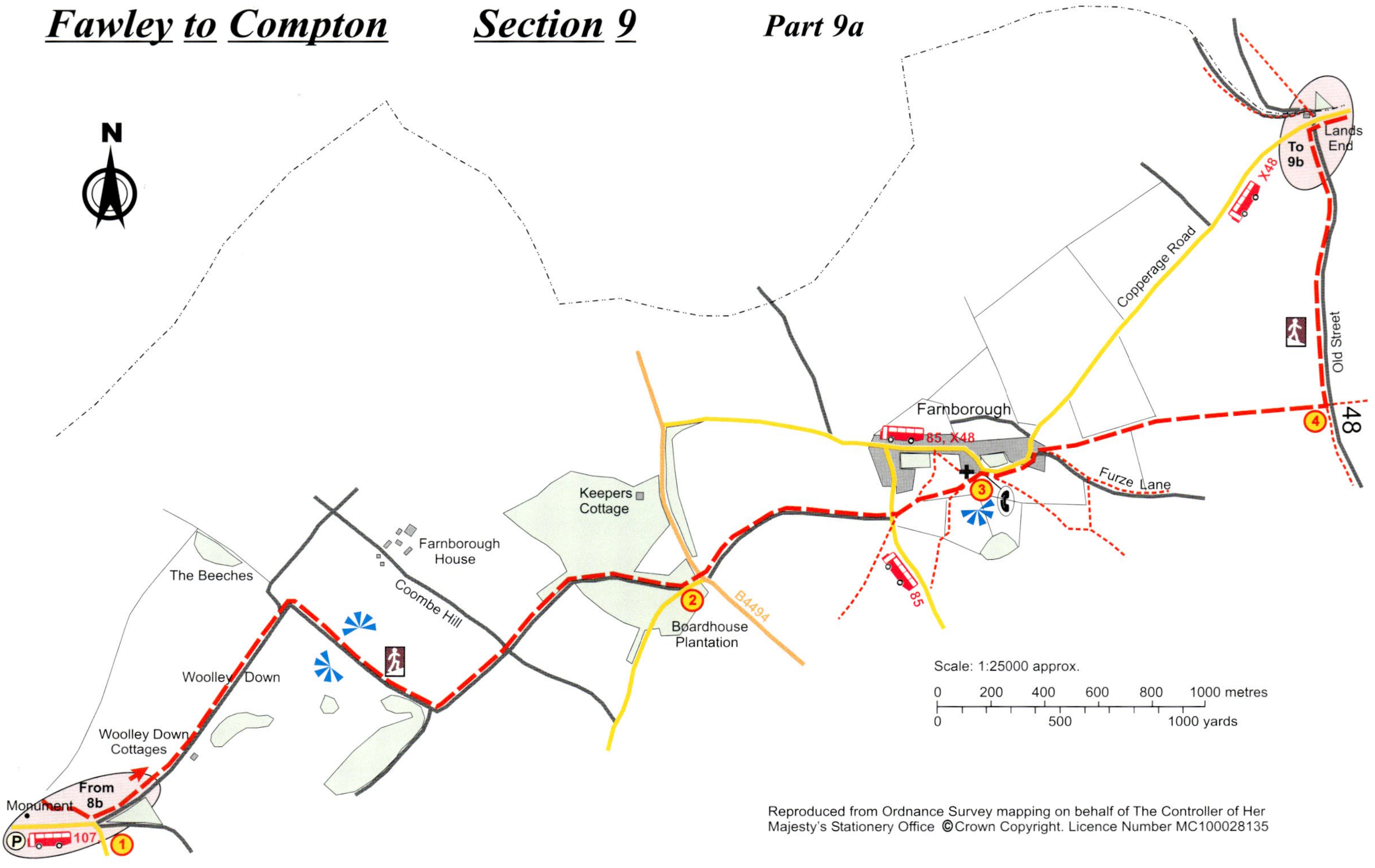

Part 9a - Fawley Monument to Lands End - About 7km (4.5ml)

This section of the Chairman's Walk takes you from the tiny downland hamlet of Fawley on through the lovely village of Farnborough, with a church window not to be missed. Old Street is aptly named and you are then introduced to the Ridgeway, both of these tracks being probably the oldest in England.

1. Turn immediately L to follow grassy track to top then R at junction with tree line on L, on grassy track. Continue in same direction up hill as path narrows to enter woods. Bear R still up hill, and continue ahead at open area on L and follow path round and bear L, still on grassy, tree lined path, to road. Cross minor grassy lane and continue in same direction through woods to Farnborough Road. *(Carpet of bluebells through woods).*

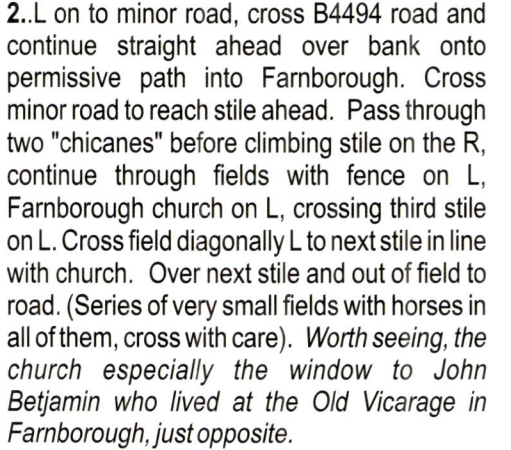

2. L on to minor road, cross B4494 road and continue straight ahead over bank onto permissive path into Farnborough. Cross minor road to reach stile ahead. Pass through two "chicanes" before climbing stile on the R, continue through fields with fence on L, Farnborough church on L, crossing third stile on L. Cross field diagonally L to next stile in line with church. Over next stile and out of field to road. (Series of very small fields with horses in all of them, cross with care). *Worth seeing, the church especially the window to John Betjamin who lived at the Old Vicarage in Farnborough, just opposite.*

3. Bear R on road, with a lovely view of the Old Vicarage on the left beyond the ha-ha.

(Gardens open to the public one afternoon in April, May and June, and it would be well worth combining the walk with a visit to the garden, details in the National Gardens Scheme Yellow Book). As road bends L, take footpath on R by the water tower, continue on grass track straight ahead, ignoring other tracks. On meeting the field, continue ahead, bearing slightly R to keep to the top of the field, rather than going down the hill.

4. On reaching the far edge of field, turn L into Old Street, reputedly the most ancient road in England. Continue down to road, turn R to walk on grass verge.

Continue on 9b

Section 9
Fawley to Compton
Part 9b

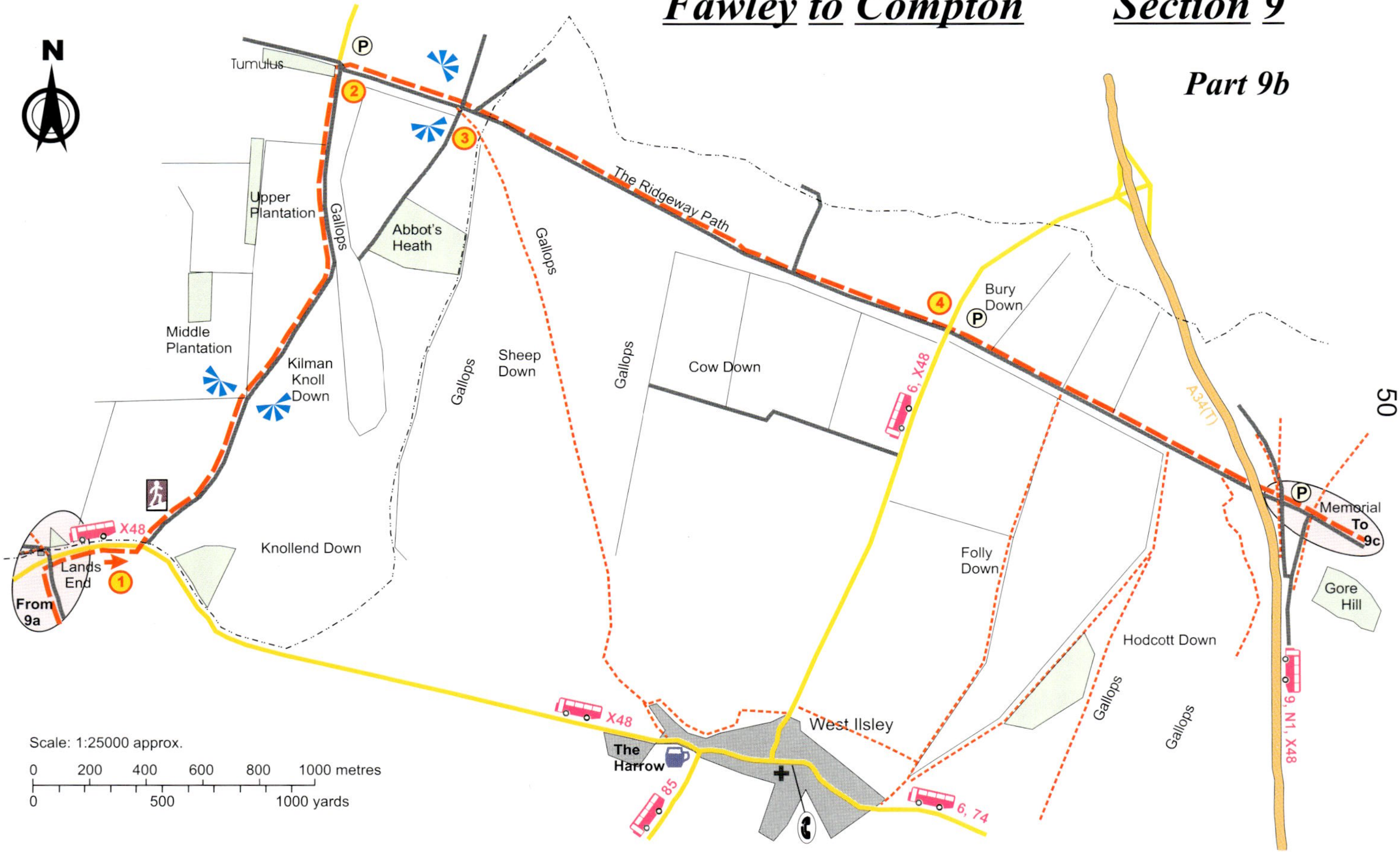

Part 9b - Lands End to Gore Hill - About 6km (3.75ml)

1. At right hand bend, cross road to track on the left which takes you on obvious chalk path up to the Ridgeway. On reaching the Ridgeway note the tumulus on the left, known locally as Scutchamer's Knob.

It is possible to walk through the village, visiting The Harrow public house and seeing the village pond with an interesting millennium project board, to then follow one of the bridleways at the Eastern end of the village back up to join the Ridgeway further along.

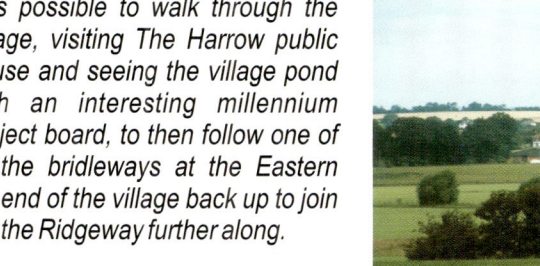

2. Turn Right. *There is a Code of Respect Notice Board at this point but you will also see the problems left by off-roaders who do not respect this.* It is possible to walk on the right hand side here to avoid the ruts.

3. After a short distance there is a bridleway by the side of the gallops which takes you into West Ilsley, one of the many pretty downland villages at the foot of the Ridgeway.

4. Our route continues along to Bury Down, where there is another large parking area. Cross the road and follow the Ridgeway to cross under the main A34 road through a tunnel in which there are murals of local scenes from days gone by painted by the local arts group. Continue ahead to reach a memorial to Hugh Frederick Grosvenor who lost his life nearby in 1947.

Continue on 9c

52

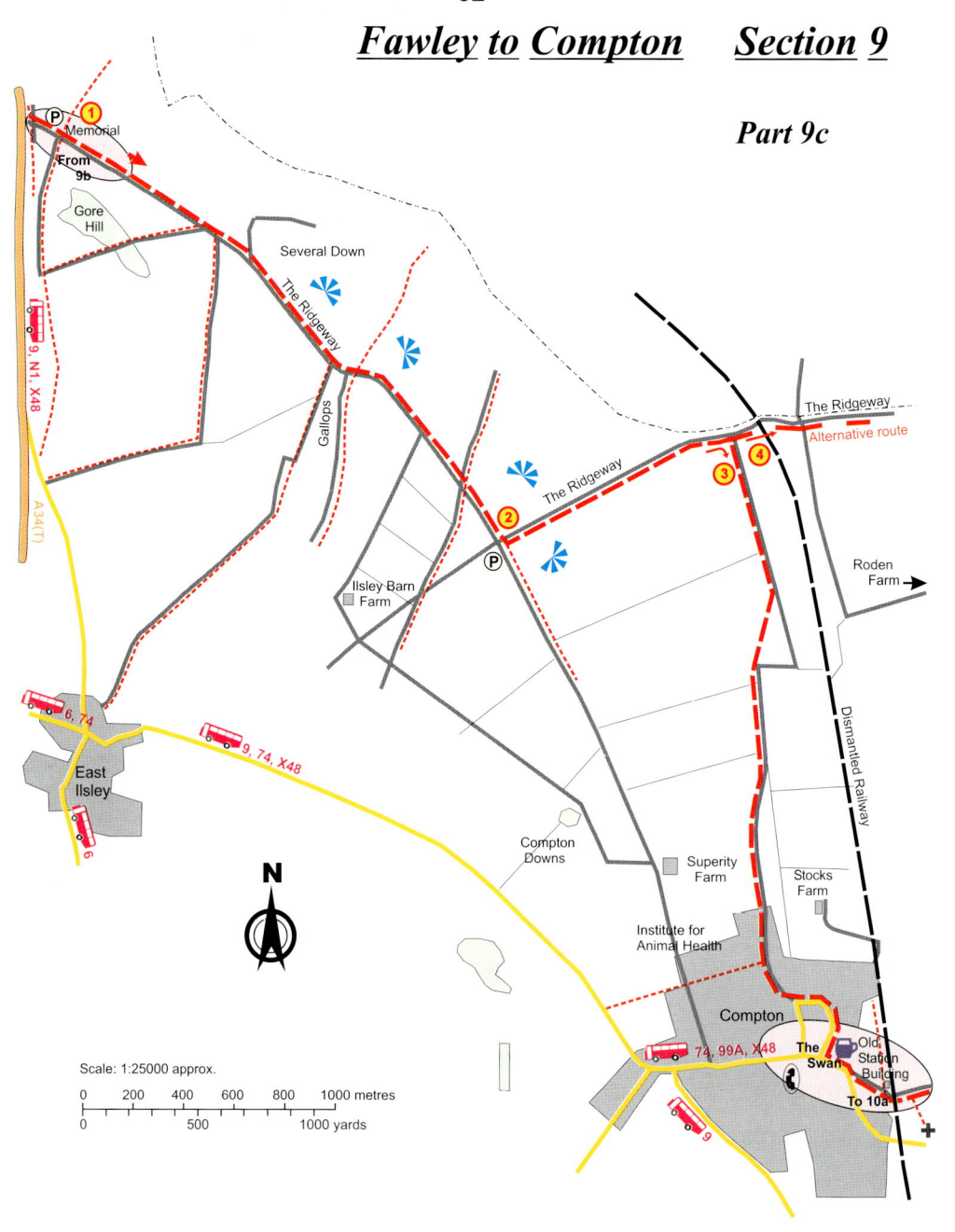

Fawley to Compton   Section 9

Part 9c

Part 9c - Gore Hill to Compton - 6km (3.75ml)

1. From the memorial continue on the Ridgeway, ignoring all turnings. (*If you wish to visit East Ilsley take second bridleway into the village where there are several pubs, a pretty downland village, and car parking around the lovely village pond. This walk can be rejoined by either walking the same way back to the Ridgeway or taking another path which leads further along the Ridgeway.*) At the Ridgeway Trail Board Code of Respect near the drinking trough and tap there is a memorial stone to Dr Basil Phillips who was a General Practitioner in Newbury who died in 1995.

2. Continuing to follow the Ridgeway signs, turn left with the Ridgeway at the concrete track. (*Views as far as Didcot Power Station on the L.*)

3. To finish section 9 in Compton take the next bridleway on the right, thereby leaving the Ridgeway. When you are opposite Roden Farm on your left, turn right through the hedge on the bridleway which goes through a gate and diagonally right across corner of the field. Bear left at the stile and continue on hedged track until meeting up with road in Compton. The Institute for Animal Health is on the right. Follow road round to the left, left at T junction, and bear right with the road to find the Compton Swan on your right in Horn Street. (*Compton is another downland village. It has a shop opposite the pub, and the landlord of The Swan is happy for walkers to park their cars in the car park by arrangement.*)

4. If you wish to continue to section 10 without visiting Compton, continue along the Ridgeway **(shown on section 10a)** over the old Didcot to Newbury railway line, bearing right where signed and following the Ridgeway signs to meet up with the path coming up from the Crows Foot and so continuing towards Streatley.

Compton to Pangbourne Section 10

Part 10a

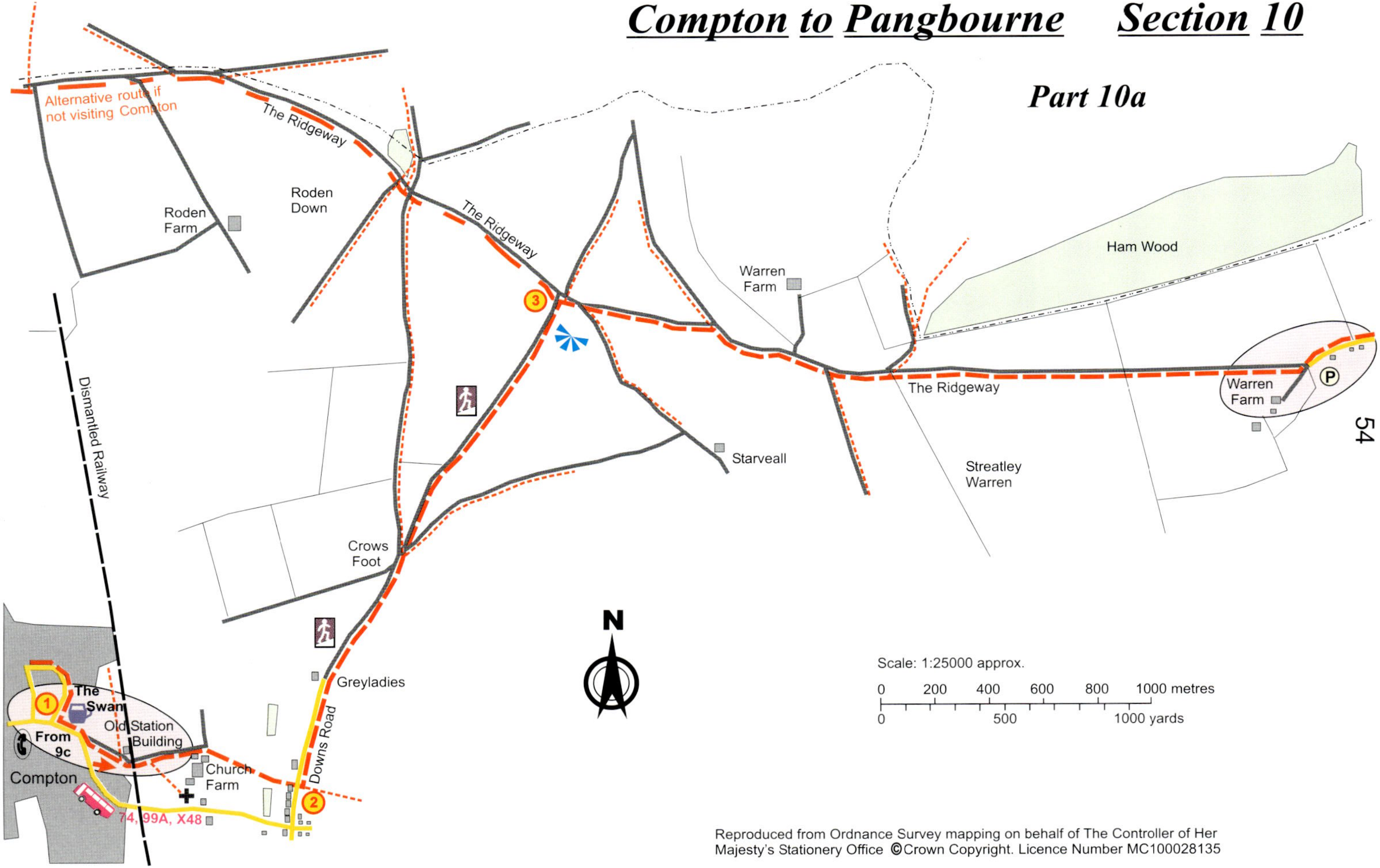

54

Part 10a - Compton to Warren Farm - About 5km (3ml)

The final section of the walk starts very close to the source of the River Pang, where it is a gulley beside School Road, Compton and ends at the mouth where it joins the River Thames at Pangbourne. In between there are fairly steep climbs on to the Ridgeway, to the top of Streatley Hill and around the edge of Harecroft Wood. All have compensating spectacular views. There is an alternative route marked which avoids one of the more testing sections. The route ends along an attractive section of the River Thames passing Beale Wildlife Park and Shooters Hill.

1. With your back to the Swan Inn turn L along School Rd, L into Wilson Close then fork L towards the old Compton railway station straight ahead. Follow footpath to R of station Building, (now a private house), cross course of disused track, down steps and into fields. Continue to L of hedge line and at farm go diagonally R across field to reach Downs Road at Glencorse.

2. Turn L and when tarmac ends continue to climb on track ahead to reach three way junction - the Crows Foot. Fork R then immediately L and continue to rejoin the Ridgeway.

3. Turn R and continue along the Ridgeway. Keep to the line of the Ridgeway ignoring all other byways and footpaths to reach Rectory Road at Post Box Cottage near Warren Farm.

Continue on 10b

Compton to Pangbourne Section 10

Part 10b

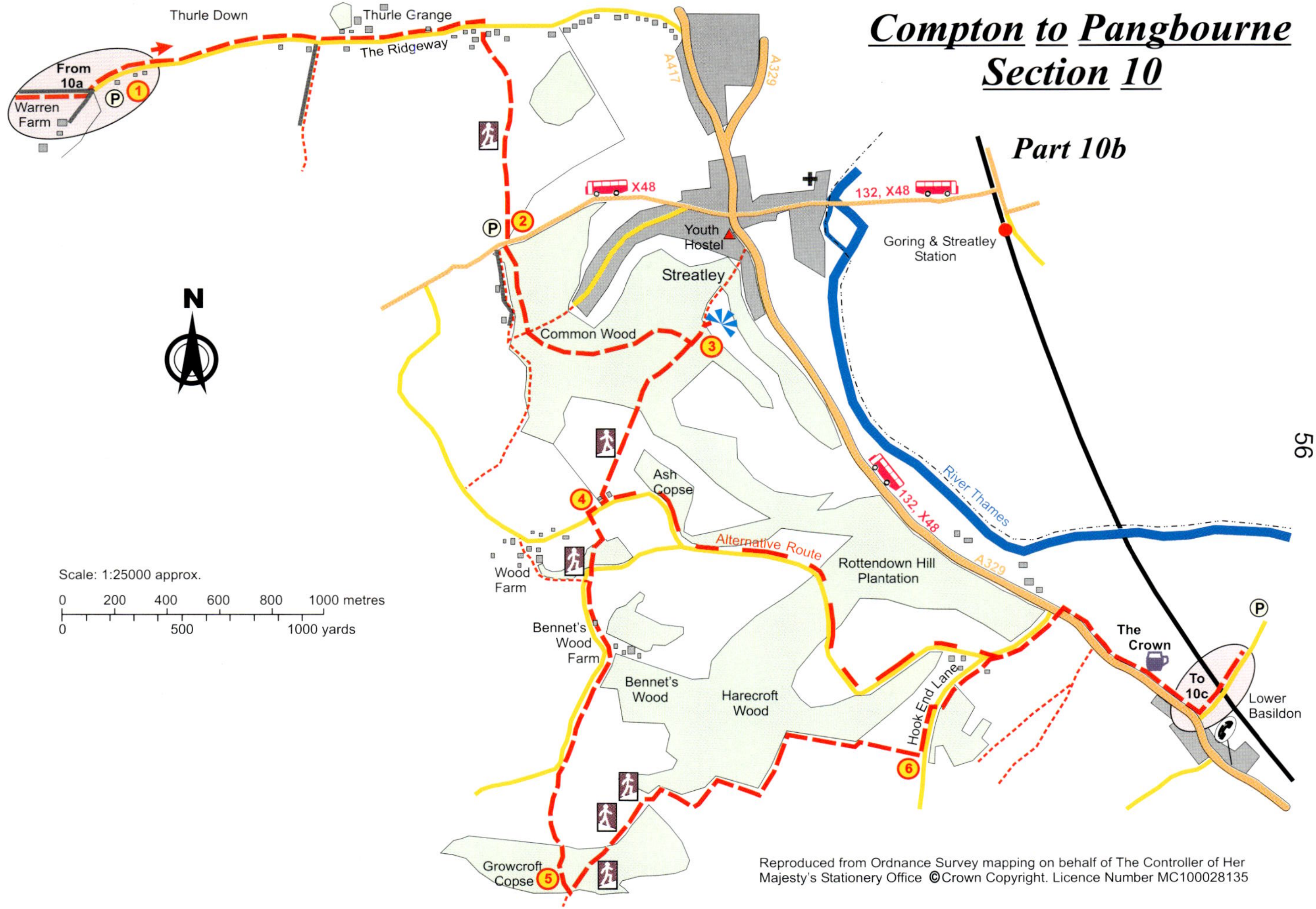

Reproduced from Ordnance Survey mapping on behalf of The Controller of Her Majesty's Stationery Office ©Crown Copyright. Licence Number MC100028135

Part 10b - Warren Farm to Lower Basildon - About 9.5km (6ml)

1. Continue along Rectory Rd. for about 1.5km (1mile) to Field Barn Farm, just after Golf Cottage. Turn R by waymark near barns to reach stile leading onto golf course. Continue up steep hill across golf course using warning bells to alert golfers, to reach National Trust car park at top of Streatley Hill.

2. Cross the road and up the steps next to National Trust 'Holies' sign to follow track through woods. Continue ahead at metal gate ignoring waymark signs to emerge at edge of meadow. With woodland on L keep to track as it swings L then R to reach stile at field edge with waymarking indicating a F/P to L & R.

3. *To get a superb panoramic view of the Thames, the villages of Goring, Streatley and the Chiltern hills beyond turn L through kissing gate and into woods for about 100m.*
Return to stile and continue on waymarked FP ahead with hedge on L to emerge at top of field. Head diagonally R across field and down slope to reach narrow lane next to house.

4. *As an alternative route to avoid some short, steep slopes and possible muddy patches, turn L along lane to reach Hook End Lane where it links again with the main route at 6 below.*

For the main route turn R at lane and after about 100m go L on FP up hill, at edge of field with hedge on R, to enter woodland at waymark on R near top of field. Turn R on reaching another lane and follow up hill as it swings to the L. About 600m after Bennet's Wood Farm and where the lane swings R, go ahead on FP (often muddy at start) which follows RH edge of field to stile in corner and down into wood.

5. At signposted cross path turn L and climb in wood to emerge into fenced path on edge of field. Enter wood at bottom of slope and after 50m bear round to R to reach field. Turn L and follow path up and down around LH edge of next two fields (FP between the two is way marked) always keeping close to tree line. At third field path descends and changes to L side of the hedge line before turning L inside field boundary for 200m to emerge into Hook End Lane.

6. Turn L along lane to reach A329. Turn R along pavement, crossing road carefully where pavement changes sides. About 200m after The Crown take narrow road on L signposted to 'Church'.

Continue on 10c

Compton to Pangbourne   Section 10

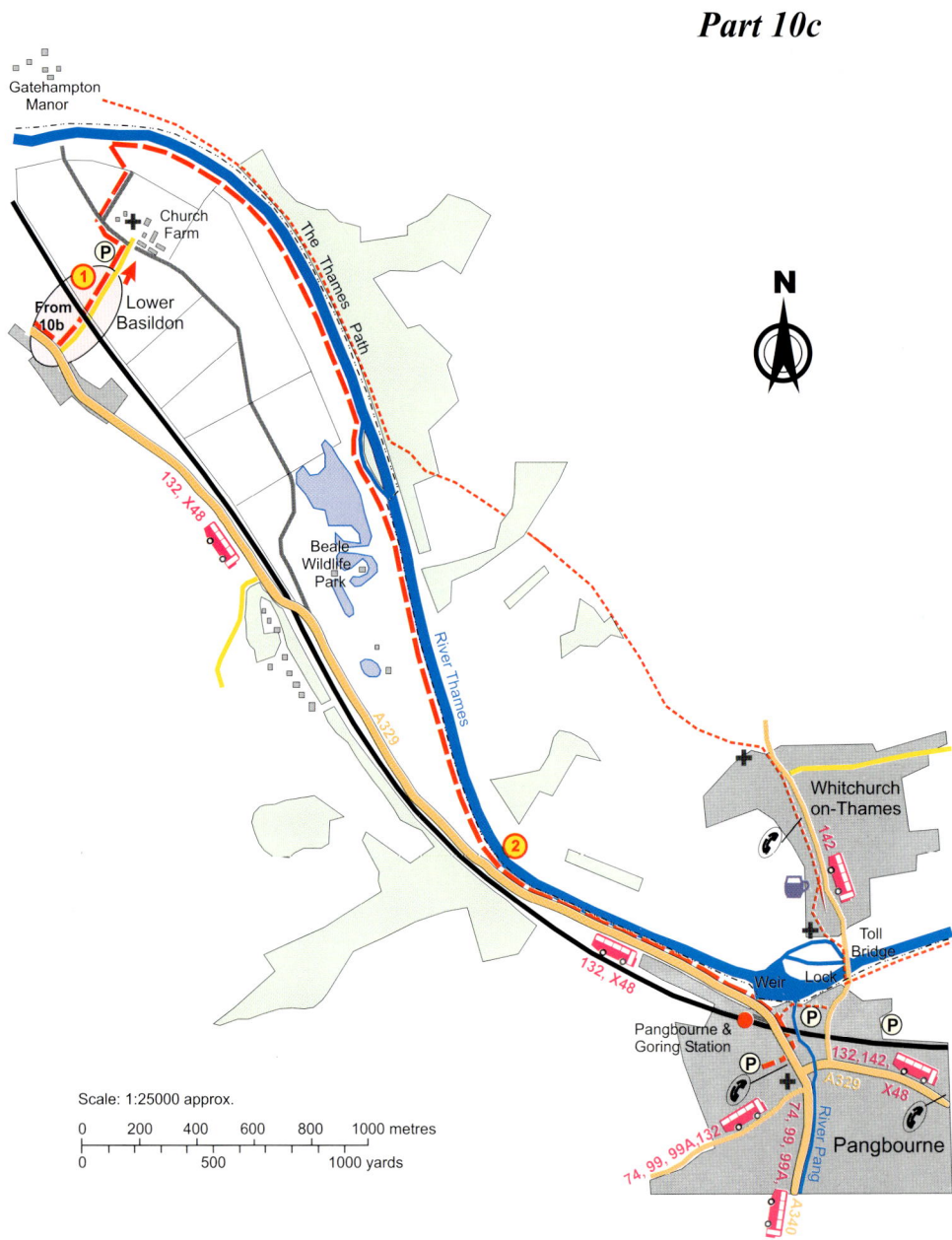

Part 10c

Part 10c - Lower Basildon to Pangbourne - About 5km (3ml)

1. Follow the narrow road across the railway line and just before the church take FP L through end of small parking area. Follow this round to the R to reach the River Thames. Turn R and walk downstream with river on your L to pass the rear entrance to Beale Park and on to meet the A329 at Shooters Hill.

2. Continue along the road to just before the railway bridge where a track to the L leads to the Adventure Dolphin Centre. The FP under the bridge leads to the main car park whilst the slope up to the R leads to Pangbourne railway station.

The end of the route.

DO YOU KNOW YOUR COUNTRY CODE?

- KEEP TO THE PATHS ACROSS FARMLAND
- FASTEN ALL GATES
- AVOID FIRES
- LEAVE NO LITTER — TAKE IT HOME
- SAFEGUARD WATER SUPPLIES
- GO CAREFULLY ON COUNTRY ROADS
- KEEP DOGS UNDER CONTROL
- AVOID DAMAGING WALLS AND FENCES
- PROTECT WILDLIFE
- RESPECT THE LIFE OF THE COUNTRYSIDE